Achieving Best Behavior for Children with Developmental Disabilities

of related interest

Anger Management
An Anger Management Training Package for Individuals with Disabilities
Hrepsime Gulbenkoglu and Nick Hagiliassis, published with Scope (Vic) Ltd
ISBN 1 84310 436 9

Homespun Remedies
Strategies in the Home and Community for Children
with Autism Spectrum and Other Disorders
Dion E. Betts and Nancy J. Patrick
ISBN 1 84310 813 5

Encouraging Appropriate Behavior for Children
on the Autism Spectrum
Frequently Asked Questions
Shira Richman
ISBN 1 84310 825 9

Assessing Behaviors Regarded as Problematic for People
with Developmental Disabilities
John Clements and Neil Martin
ISBN 1 85302 998 X

Assessing and Developing Communication and Thinking Skills
in People with Autism and Communication Difficulties
A Toolkit for Parents and Professionals
Kate Silver, Autism Initiatives
ISBN 1 84310 352 4

Parenting the ADD Child
Can't Do? Won't Do? Practical Strategies for Managing Behaviour
Problems in Children with ADD and ADHD
David Pentecost
ISBN 1 85302 811 8

People with Autism Behaving Badly
Helping People with ASD Move On from Behavioral
and Emotional Challenges
John Clements
ISBN 1 84310 765 1

Social Skills Training for Adolescents with General Moderate
Learning Difficulties
Ursula Cornish and Fiona Ross
ISBN 1 84310 179 3

Kids in the Syndrome Mix of ADHD, LD, Asperger's, Tourette's,
Bipolar, and More!
The one stop guide for parents, teachers, and other professionals
Martin L. Kutscher MD, with contributions from Tony Attwood PhD and Robert R. Wolff MD
ISBN 1 84310 810 0 hb
ISBN 1 84310 811 9 pb

Achieving Best Behavior for Children with Developmental Disabilities

A Step-By-Step Workbook for Parents and Carers

Pamela Lewis

Jessica Kingsley Publishers
London and Philadelphia

First published in 2006
by Jessica Kingsley Publishers
116 Pentonville Road
London N1 9JB, UK
and
400 Market Street, Suite 400
Philadelphia, PA 19106, USA

www.jkp.com

Index by Indexing Specialists (UK) Ltd, Hove.

British Library Cataloguing in Publication Data
A CIP catalogue record for this book is available from the British Library

ISBN-13: 978 1 84310 809 2
ISBN-10: 1 84310 809 7

Printed and bound in Great Britain by
Athenaeum Press, Gateshead, Tyne and Wear

11/2/09

*This book is dedicated to the individuals
with developmental disabilities and their families
with whom I have had the privilege of working,
and from whom I have learned so much.*

Acknowledgements

I appreciate the opportunity I have had to work with many highly skilled and dedicated colleagues for the past nine years at the Waisman Center, University of Wisconsin at Madison. In particular, I thank Susan Heighway, Anne Heintzelman, and Rae Sprague for reviewing portions of the manuscript. I also thank the Autism Society of Wisconsin for posting an earlier version of the manuscript on their website, which allowed me to receive many helpful suggestions. I thank the many individuals who wrote to me at that time with their feedback. The book has benefited from all of their suggestions, but the responsibility for any flaws is entirely my own.

Contents

Introduction

Intended audience

Although this book is written in language aimed at parents of children with a developmental disability such as autism and/or intellectual disability, the basic principles apply to adults as well as children, and the book can be used by others involved with a child or adult with a developmental disability, for example, teachers, school psychologists, occupational therapists, physical therapists, speech/language therapists, social workers, case managers with governmental agencies responsible for individuals with developmental disabilities, residential staff in group homes for adults with developmental disabilities, and vocational staff or job coaches working with adults with developmental disabilities.

It could also be used by a parent and professional together, to develop plans for addressing behavior in a person with a developmental disability.

Goal of the book

Parenting is a demanding enterprise. Parenting children with developmental disabilities can be yet more demanding. Although basic principles apply to all children, it can be more challenging to apply some of these principles when a child has a developmental disability. It is the aim of this book to help you understand these principles and how to apply them with your child, so that you can experience more of the rewards of parenting and fewer of the frustrations.

Format of the book

The book is presented in an interactive workbook format, so that you can move toward this general goal in small, concrete steps. The book is based on the premise that achieving skill is a developmental process. It is important to understand the individual's levels of development, to start at that point and move ahead slowly, with frequent successes and encouragement all along the way. This is true whether we are talking about developing your child's skills or your own.

Structure and content of the book

Each section begins with some discussion of the issue, and then has exercises for you to do related to that material. The book begins with some preliminaries. Perhaps the first and most important step is to start thinking of yourself as someone who can have a very positive impact on your child and his or her behavior, even if you don't feel this has been the case thus far. This workbook is designed to give you the skills you need. Another important step is to rule out any physical/medical causes for your child's behavior. It is also important to gather or create a support system around you, so you will have the energy to do this important work. Finally, there is an overview of the main ideas to be developed in the book.

After these preliminaries, the book covers how to understand your child's developmental levels, how to define behavior, the many functions of behavior, and how to develop a plan for one specific behavior. The process can then be repeated with additional behaviors, if desired.

At the end of the book are some strategies for common dilemmas, such as haircuts, going shopping or to restaurants, and going to visit friends. You can flip to those right away if you recognize a situation. There is also an appendix with ideas for rewards/reinforcers, and another appendix of resources on autism and intellectual disability.

Note

The child will be referred to as either "he" or "she" throughout this book. There is no intention to portray some situations or behaviors as more typical of boys than girls, or vice versa.

Disclaimer

The advice given is believed to be the best generic advice possible, but neither the author nor the publisher can take responsibility for specific outcomes.

PART I

STARTING OUT

1

Believe You Can

Before we get started, it is important for you to examine your feelings and attitudes toward yourself in the role of someone who can help your child to have more positive behavior. It is important to believe you can do it, otherwise you may not give your efforts the energy and commitment needed to succeed.

Raising a child with a developmental disability is challenging

It's often more difficult to deal with the behavior of a child with developmental disabilities compared to that of a typically developing child. Parenting skills that would be more than adequate for a typically developing child may not be enough, that is, you may need to learn a few additional skills to help life run more smoothly. You may make a few mistakes with a typically developing child, and they still "get" it. Everyone makes some mistakes in parenting. But with a child with special needs, your mistakes may "cost" more. It's not fair, but that is often the way it is.

You are an expert on your child

Simply by living with your child you have learned a great deal about her, and you probably know more than anyone else about her. This knowledge is extremely valuable. It will help you design successful behavior plans.

Don't lose faith in yourself

Don't lose faith in yourself if you find yourself challenged by a child with special needs. Most people are. It does not reflect on you. It's a reflection of the fact that you're dealing with a more challenging situation than most parents have to face.

Anyone can master behavior principles

The basic behavior principles that will be discussed here are not magic. They are not rocket science. They are simple to understand, although not always simple to implement. It may take some experimenting, and fine-tuning, *but they work!* For example, consider rewards, something that will be discussed a great deal in this book. People sometimes say that rewards do not work with their child. Rewards always work, by definition, because a reward is something that increases the behavior preceding it, but the trick may be to discover what is rewarding for some children.

You are not alone

There are resources available, and people and places to support you. In section 3, we will discuss how to identify or create your support network.

Believe you can

The fears that I have about my ability to deal with my child's behavior (e.g., that I'm not skilled enough, not patient enough, that my child doesn't care, that I can't do it alone, etc.):

What I can tell myself when I feel those fears arise (e.g., the points made above):

What I can do when those fears arise (e.g., find a way to take a break, talk to someone who believes in me, etc.):

Some examples of times when I felt good about how I handled my child's behavior are (if you think you have nothing to put here, think again; you may not have looked hard enough; give yourself credit, even if it seems small compared to experiences with typically developing children):

2

Medical Factors

When considering what to do about your child's undesirable behaviors it is important that you first rule out medical factors. Discuss your child's behavior with your pediatrician to make sure that there are no medical conditions which could be causing or contributing to your child's behavior. Regular dental care is important as well.

Any pain or discomfort could cause a child's behavior to be more negative than it would otherwise be. Just to give a few examples (*not* a complete list): headaches, allergies, some kinds of seizures, gastroesophageal reflux, ulcers, hemorrhoids, constipation, oral and dental problems (e.g., cavities, gum disease, abscesses), and tiredness could all lead to tantrums or other negative behaviors. For females, gynecological problems such as vaginal infections or monthly periods can cause discomfort and lead to negative behaviors. For example, a young woman who had autism and was nonverbal had bouts of aggression and self-abuse that were found to be cyclical and occurred with her menstrual period. Because she was nonverbal, she could not tell anyone that she was in pain. Pain medication given at those times eliminated the behavior. Similarly a little boy, who was also nonverbal, was having frequent tantrums. His dentist discovered an abscessed tooth. This was not visible just by looking inside his mouth. Medical intervention eliminated the behavior.

Many dentists are not prepared to see children with developmental disabilities, many of whom may require sedation for routine work. You may need to consult with your local autism organization or society to find a dentist who can see your child (see Appendix 2).

Also consider the side effects of any medications your child may be taking. For example, some medications might cause restlessness, some can make a child thirstier than usual, some might make it difficult to sleep, and some can cause constipation.

Lack of sleep for any reason could have an impact on behavior. See the section in Part VI, page 126 on helping your child stay calm. Some of those strategies could be helpful at bedtime to promote a good night's sleep. See also *Sleep Better! A Guide to Improving Sleep for Children with Special Needs* by V. Mark Durand. Hunger and thirst can have an impact on behavior, so it's important to know when your child is eating and drinking, as well as having bowel movements (to rule out constipation).

Possible medical factors

My child's last physical/check-up was (date):
I discussed the following behaviors with my pediatrician:

My child takes the following medications:

Possible side effects include:

My child's last dental exam was (date):
Findings:

My child has the following allergies (if any):

My child's sleep schedule is (how many hours per night, on average):

My child eats and drinks on the following schedule (approximate times of meals, snacks, and having something to drink):

Physical factors that can affect behavior

Which of the following could be factors in your child's behavior?

Pain/discomfort

- ☐   Dental
- ☐   Gastrointestinal (stomach ache, reflux, ulcers, etc.)
- ☐   Joints/muscles
- ☐   Headache
- ☐   Ears
- ☐   Eyes
- ☐   Lungs
- ☐   Menstrual
- ☐   Other gynecological
- ☐   Other

☐ Allergies

☐ Medication side effects (specify):

☐ Hunger

☐ Thirst

☐ Tiredness

☐ Illness (cold, stomach flu, etc.)

Signals

I can tell when my child is tired by:

I can tell when my child is hungry by:

I can tell when my child is thirsty by:

I can tell when my child is ill by:

I can tell when my child is uncomfortable/in pain by:

If my child is able to communicate about discomfort/pain, he or she does so by:

- ☐ verbalizing
- ☐ asking for something in particular
- ☐ signing
- ☐ using gestures, such as pointing to where it hurts
- ☐ pointing to a picture of a face representing someone in pain
- ☐ other

Your child may not be able to tell you about her discomfort. Even typically developing children do not always know when they are tired and sick, so you need to be able to read your child's signals.

Teach your child to communicate about discomfort

You might try coaching your child to use some of the above methods, if he doesn't already. First, determine the best mode for communication for your child. If he rarely talks, pick gestures or pictures. If sign language has been unsuccessful in the past, or if fine motor skills are challenging, use pictures.

Use pictures of a child yawning, drinking, eating, or looking like he is in pain. When you discover what is bothering your child, show him the picture and pair it with the word (e.g., "thirsty"). Have the pictures available, e.g., on the refrigerator door, so that eventually your child can get the picture and bring it to you to communicate what he is feeling.

If he is able to sign, have him make the sign for "thirsty" as you give him the glass of water.

To help him verbalize that something hurts, for example, repeat the word "hurts" in situations in which you know he has hurt himself and is distressed by it. An example might be when he has just scraped his knee or banged himself.

Sometimes it works best to use all modes together, or at least more than one, for example, showing the picture of the child in pain and saying the word "hurts" whenever the appropriate situation arises.

Communicating discomfort

The mode or modes that will work best for my child are:

I will do the following to help my child communicate about discomfort (e.g., make a set of pictures and post on the refrigerator):

3

Identify or Create Your Support Network

Living with a child with a disability can be stressful and it can sap your energy. Developing and implementing behavior plans takes time and energy. Where will you get the energy to do all this? How will you maintain your motivation? The answer is that you need support. If you don't have a support network already, you can create one. This section will give you some ideas on how to do this, even if you don't think it's possible. It's not selfish to create this for yourself. Not only do you deserve it, but so does your child: you can't give anything to your child if you're running on empty yourself!

Your support network can give you many important things. Not everyone in your support network will necessarily provide everything, but you may get different things from different people.

Kinds of support

Emotional support

Someone to talk to, someone to provide encouragement and validate the efforts you are making; someone to share the hard times and the good times; they may or may not have personal experience with raising a child with a developmental disability.

Understanding

Someone who's been there and understands what you're talking about; someone who does know personally what it's like to raise a child with a developmental disability.

Advice

Someone who can give suggestions and advice on behavior, purchasing certain kinds of equipment or toys, how to explain your child's disability to others, to name just a few things.

Practical help

For example, someone to provide you with a break, or to help you with your child when you take him or her to the grocery store or to the doctor.

There are many places where you can look to develop your support network As you do this, remember that you are not just asking for something, but *offering* something, as well. Most of us enjoy being helpful to others, so you are providing the opportunity to be helpful. Furthermore, many people enjoy children and would like to learn more about children with disabilities.

Sources of support

Family

Is everyone pitching in? Are there issues in the family that need to be addressed? This could be a book in itself. Define what you want from other family members and then have a discussion with them about it. Consider counseling if you would like assistance in planning and having this discussion. Individual counseling can help you identify and assert your needs. Couple and family counseling can help in communicating with each other to negotiate a win-win solution. Sometimes when issues are long-standing it is very challenging to know what to do without the views and advice of an outside party who does not have a history with the issues or personal investment in them.

Extended family

Does your extended family understand your child's disability? Do you need to spend some time educating them and letting them know how they could help? (See the section below on educating others about your child's disability, page 23.) Do members of your extended family live close by? If not, or even if they do and they don't want to help baby-sit, would they be willing to pitch in to pay for a baby-sitter once a month, or buy some special toy that would be helpful?

Friends

Do your friends understand your child's disability? Do you need to spend some time educating them and letting them know how they could help? (See the section below on educating others about your child's disability, page 23.) They may also be willing to trade child care with you, if they have some specific information on how to deal with your child. Sometimes people feel uncomfortable because they can't fix the problem. It may help them to know that just listening helps you, and you may decide to tell them that explicitly.

Your child's school

Have you talked to your child's teacher? Are there other professionals at the school who are helpful, such as the school nurse, social worker, your child's therapists, school psychologist, director of special education, principal, etc.? There may be someone at your child's school who could work with you as you use this workbook.

Other parents of a child with a disability

Have you joined parent organizations related to your child's disability? These can be a tremendous source of support. Have you asked your child's teacher for ideas on how to meet other parents? (Maybe he or she could have a "parent night" some time.) Also see Appendix 2, page 148.

Respite through your county's developmental disabilities agency

In many states in the US, respite and other services are available through your county developmental disabilities agency. The waiting list is usually long, so it's important to get on the list as soon as possible. Many parents are not comfortable with leaving their child with a stranger. Remember that you can get to know a respite worker, so they won't always be a stranger! You don't have to actually leave your child alone with them until you are comfortable with it. They can come to your home while you are there, at first.

Neighbors

Do your neighbors understand your child's disability? Do you need to spend some time educating them, and letting them know how they could be helpful? (See the section below on educating others, page 23.)

Churches, synagogues, mosques and other religious institutions

Even if you're not a member, consider asking if there are members who would like to do some volunteer work, e.g., baby-sit, or just come by to play with your child and give you a break.

Volunteer centers

You can make the same request of volunteer centers. Check with your local library, and/or look in the yellow pages of your phone book under "volunteer organizations".

Local colleges — psychology, special education departments, and so on

Many students are considering careers in the field of developmental disabilities and would love the opportunity to spend time with your child!

Internet

There are now many websites and chat groups on the internet devoted to children with disabilities. Be discriminating and look for sites sponsored by reputable organizations. (See Appendix 2 for some good organizations.)

Inner resources

We all need support from others, but we also need support from within. One important purpose of your support network is to allow you time to do the things that help you re-energize, e.g., soaking in a tub, reading a good book, meditating, playing sports, pursuing a hobby, talking to friends, having time to just "smell the roses," attending religious services, etc.

Educating others about your child's disability

Educating family and others involved with the child

For those who are interested, there are many informative and engrossing books about children with disabilities (see Appendix 2). For those who don't want to read a lot of books, you may want to prepare a simple "fact sheet," including such information as:

1. The name of the disability and its prevalence.

2. Common characteristics and behaviors.

3. Reasons for unusual behaviors, e.g.,
   ○ Children with autism may insist on order and routine because it gives them a sense of security.
   ○ Children with autism may have difficulty making friends because they have trouble understanding social cues and because they have language delays.

- Children with intellectual disabilities may take longer to generalize what they have learned.
- Children with intellectual disabilities need more repetition and concrete examples in order to learn.
- Children with intellectual disabilities may not be able to succeed in advanced high school and college courses.

4. Your child's likes, dislikes, and fears.

5. How to respond to your child's specific challenging behaviors, e.g.,
   - Give Johnny choices rather than making demands, whenever possible.
   - If Johnny has a tantrum, remove him to a quiet place and talk soothingly, while preventing him from injuring himself or others.

These are just some suggestions, but you will probably want to design your own fact sheet. Internet websites can be a great source of basic information. Go to the website for the specific syndrome your child has (enter the name of it into a search engine), or go to the websites for autism and/or intellectual disabilities. (See the list in Appendix 2.) Make sure the websites are sponsored by reputable organizations.

Educating members of the general public whom you encounter

One thing you can do, which some families have found very useful, is to make many copies of a card (about the size of a business card) with basic information on it. You can then hand this card to strangers who may give disapproving looks or unsolicited advice. It saves you the trouble of having a discussion at a critical time when you need to be dealing with your child. It also lets people know that parenting is not the issue and provides needed public education. Some families include ways for people to help at challenging times, if they wish. Most people are eager to help when they understand the situation. Some children with developmental disabilities may be very attractive and not look like there is anything unusual about them; therefore, it may be especially hard for outsiders to understand what is really going on.

An example of such a card might be: "My child may look entirely normal, but he has Autistic Disorder, a neurodevelopmental disorder affecting learning, language, and emotional responses. He has an obsessive interest in pens and every time we go any place where there are pens he will try to grab all that are in sight. When prevented from doing this he has an intense tantrum. If you want to help, you can assist me with carrying my packages while I get him to the car."

My plan for developing my support network

My present support network consists of the following people:

and the following organizations:

I would like to find support for the following (e.g., respite, emotional support, practical advice, other parents who understand, etc.):

I have identified the following individuals to approach with the goal of further developing my support network:

and the following places/agencies (don't forget your child's school):

4

Overview

There are three key things *you* can do that will improve your child's behavior:

1.   Notice and respond to the positive behaviors your child has.

2.   Have appropriate expectations for your child, so you can reward positive behavior frequently, and naturally.

3.   Make sure there is fun in your child's life and yours.

These will be discussed in more detail later, but here is a quick introduction.

Notice and respond to positive behaviors

What we pay attention to often becomes our reality. The behaviors we attend to in our child tend to increase and hence inceasingly define our child. This is true only to some extent because there are real challenges for children with special needs, apart from how parents and others respond. The way parents and others respond can, however, have a big impact.

Most people notice the negative behaviors their child has, because these are the behaviors that are upsetting. Their attention zeroes in on the problem behavior. This is natural and normal, but two things can happen as a result, neither of which helps your child's behavior to improve:

1.   The negative behavior may increase because this is what you are attending to. Attention is usually rewarding, even if it is negative attention in the form of scolding, yelling, etc.

2.   You overlook, and fail to build upon, the positive behaviors you would like to see instead.

For example, let's say Joey, a five-year-old with autism, is playing with a puzzle on the living room floor. He is fiddling with the pieces but putting one in occasionally. After 15 minutes he gets up and goes over to the living room curtains and starts pulling them down. His mother runs over and tells him not to do that. She then tries to redirect him to the puzzle, but he is determined to grab the curtains. A battle ensues, and Joey is put in time-out. What has Joey learned?

Joey has learned that when he is doing a puzzle and not playing with the curtains, no one pays any attention. Mom does not appear to value that behavior. When he pulls at the curtains, however, he gets lots of attention from mom, and a stimulating scenario ensues. When he is bored and uncertain what to do next, pulling the curtains brings a predictable and exciting result.

You may be thinking you can't go around rewarding your child's behavior every five minutes, in order to avoid misbehavior. That leads us to the second point.

Have appropriate expectations

Level of functioning

A child behaves best when success is attainable and rewarded. If expectations are too high or too low, behavior may become challenging.

No one likes to be bored, and no one likes to be frustrated. You would not enjoy watching a purple cartoon dinosaur sing and dance for a half-hour, because it would be too boring. It's not challenging for you. A three-year-old, however, might enjoy that because she is at a different cognitive level. On the other hand, you would not enjoy listening to a highly technical lecture on particle physics, either, unless that is your specialty, because it would be too difficult to understand. It would become boring. Your level of understanding is not that of a particle physicist.

More often than not, children's behavior becomes difficult because what is being expected of them is not at their level. People often don't realize what is required for a child with special needs to perform a task or respond to a demand, and they expect too much. Expecting too much is far more common than expecting too little.

In the example above, Joey may not yet be capable of entertaining himself independently for more than 10–15 minutes. He needs to have some alternative activities ready for him when he tires of the puzzle. Rewarding him every five minutes may not be feasible, but it might be possible to reward him every ten minutes with a quick "nice playing!" or "good for you!" along with a raisin or other reward some of the time if praise alone is not effective.

Whenever you think you don't have time to reward behavior, remember that the alternative is usually dealing with misbehavior. Dealing with the misbehavior often ends up taking much more time than rewarding the positive behavior. The trick is to find quick and easily dispensed rewards. This will be discussed in more detail in section 13.

Level of functioning may vary across skill areas

Another factor to consider is that many children with special needs have peaks and valleys in their abilities. We all have things we are good at and things we're not so skilled at, but for children with special needs, the profile of strengths and weaknesses is often more exaggerated than usual. They may be quite good at some things and have significant difficulties with others. Because they are good at some things, people may assume they are good at everything and are just not trying. Level of functioning may vary, so your expectations may need to vary as well.

For example, many children with autism are very good at doing puzzles and figuring out how mechanical things work. A child with autism may work the VCR better than his parents! Yet he may have trouble understanding verbal directions, or buttoning buttons. This is who he is. Who he is includes the very individual, unique profile of strengths and weaknesses that he has.

Level of functioning may vary across time

Yet another factor is that we all have good days and bad days. We all have times when everything "clicks" and we can do things that we usually can't. Because your child did something on one occasion, don't hold him to that standard all the time.

Back down!

Instead of saying "I *know* she can do it," and getting frustrated with your child, try backing down a little. Break the task into smaller parts, help your child to get the task started, provide some "hints" or other support, use a picture schedule of the steps, provide a structured setting, embed the task in a routine, use rewards as incentives, etc., and see what happens. For example, instead of giving her a two- or three-part direction, give her one part at a time. Use a picture or other visual cue to support the verbal direction. If she has trouble buttoning, get the button started for her and see whether she can push the button the rest of the way through the hole. If she makes a mess eating meals, ask the occupational therapist about adaptive spoons to help her accomplish feeding more easily. If she doesn't play a game by herself, play it with her for several days and then fade yourself out slowly. If she still doesn't learn the game, then try a simpler game, or simplify the game you have been using. These kinds of suggestions will be discussed in more detail throughout this workbook.

Make sure there is fun in your child's life and yours

To put fun in your child's life you must first find things that are fun for your child. No one is likely to behave well if they are never having any fun. Some children with developmental disabilities do not have acceptable ways of entertaining themselves. They may frequently get into trouble. Life for them may be a series of "no"s and "stop"s. There will be discussion of ways to build leisure skills later on in this book (see pages 78–79.)

If *you* are not having any fun, then go back to section 3, on identifying or creating your support network. You can't do all the things you need to do for your child if you are never having any fun. Fun helps you re-energize!

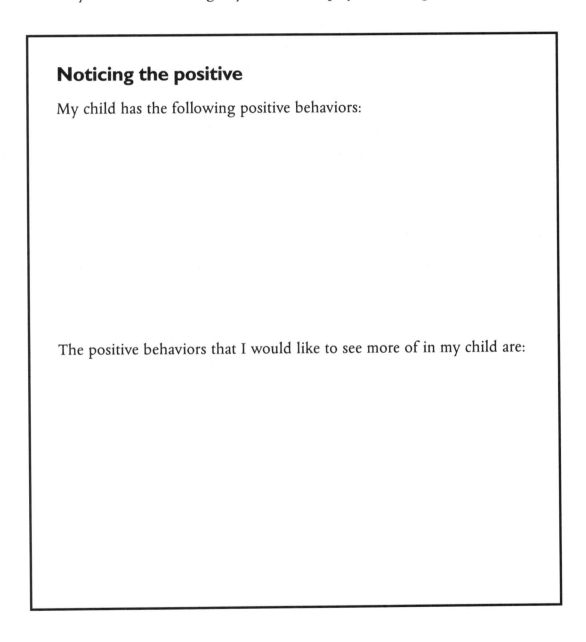

Noticing the positive

My child has the following positive behaviors:

The positive behaviors that I would like to see more of in my child are:

See page 28 for some examples of ways you could "back down"; list the area of difficulty and the way to back down in that area. You may find it helpful to talk to your child's teacher about this. Some examples:

1. My child does not follow two-step directions.

   Ways to back down: Give directions one at a time; show a picture of the object or activity I want him to get/do; gently start him in the direction of what I want him to do using hand-over-hand guidance.

2. My child does not play by herself.

   Ways to back down: Provide toys one at a time; teach her how to play with a few specific toys; limit the time she is expected to play alone and allow videos at other times; find a neighbor or college student to play with her some of the time.

3. My child does not bathe independently.

   Ways to back down: Consider his level of motor development and plan on providing assistance until he is more mature; provide hand-over-hand guidance if he is mature enough motorically to progress in this area (you might want to talk to your child's occupational therapist about this).

Appropriate expectations

My child is good at (think about expressive language, understanding language, motor, social, mechanical, visual, thinking skills, etc.):

My child has trouble with (think about those same areas):

Ways to back down

In the space below, write some examples of things that are challenging for your child and ways you could back down. (This will be discussed in more detail later on so you may get other ideas as you continue reading.)

Fun

Things my child enjoys are (think of things he likes to do, toys, games, videos, TV shows, sensory stimulation, etc. Include things that are not considered socially appropriate but that your child really enjoys. See the section on seeking sensory stimulation to discover substitute activities that may be more appropriate.):

PART II

UNDERSTAND YOUR CHILD'S DEVELOPMENTAL LEVELS

5

Developmental Levels

Understanding your child's abilities and working with him at his level is critical. No one wants to be in over their head. Imagine going to a cooking or craft demonstration and being unable to mimic with your own materials what the teacher is doing; or attending a highly technical lecture and being unable to comprehend it or even recognize some of the vocabulary; asking a question of someone at a social gathering and getting a long-winded answer that does not seem to even relate to the question you asked. Everyone learns best when approached at their ability level, with expectations to slowly and incrementally increase their ability. Understanding your child's developmental levels is critical, so you can start where he is and proceed from there.

Note that this section is about "developmental levels," plural, not just one "developmental level." You must look at the different areas of development and find the level for *each* area, rather than look for one single developmental level. Some of the areas of development that are most commonly described are: speech (clearly articulating sounds), language (e.g., using and understanding grammar and vocabulary), fine motor (skill in using the fingers or other smaller muscles of the body, e.g., using a pencil, picking up small objects, unscrewing lids), visual-motor (coordinating motor skills with sight, as in copying work from a book or from the board), gross motor (skill in using larger muscles, e.g., running and jumping), cognitive (thinking), attention, social, and self-care/independent living skills. Developmental levels often vary widely across these areas, in a child with a developmental disability. This is why it is often not useful to think in terms of a single developmental level for a child.

It is often assumed that because a child is good, or relatively good, in one area, they are good in all the other areas, as well. If they don't do well in one of these other areas, they are believed to be "lazy" or "just not trying." More often, the child simply has a profile of skills with peaks and valleys: they are very good at some things and not very good at others. Everyone is like this to some extent, but the peaks and valleys are sometimes more pronounced in children with developmental disabilities.

In specific learning situations, people tend to expect too much of children with developmental disabilities more often than they expect too little. For example, a child's silence or inattention are assumed to be signs of boredom (i.e., the work is so easy it's boring him), without evidence to support this belief. In general, it's easy to back down and make it simpler. Often the results are very positive. Consider whether the following points apply to your child.

- If your child's disability includes speech skills, he or she may have difficulty articulating certain sounds or combinations of sounds.

- If your child's disability includes language skills, she may have more difficulty understanding directions than a typical child of the same age. Speech/language therapists recommend that *your* utterances be no more than double the length of your *child's* typical utterance. She may also have difficulty with expressing herself via language, for example, she may have trouble putting together a sentence to express a thought, even when you feel she knows what she would like to say.

- If your child's disability includes fine motor skills, she may have more difficulty managing buttons, zippers, and eating utensils, and using a pencil to write, than a typical child of the same age.

- If your child's disability includes visual-motor skills, she may have trouble placing pegs in a pegboard, copying from a board, copying from a book, playing catch, kickball or volleyball, or jumping rope.

- If your child's disability includes gross motor skills, she may have difficulty with understanding her position in space (hence tending to bump into things and people), running, jumping, and participating in sports. Balancing and sitting or standing in one place for any length of time may be difficult.

- If your child's disability includes cognitive skills, she may have more difficulty generalizing skills to new situations, understanding basic concepts (yes/no, same/different, before/after, if-then, later, next, now, etc.), problem-solving in new situations, and remembering things.

- If your child's disability includes the development of attention, she may have trouble paying attention. She may also have difficulties organizing herself when performing a task, initiating a task, remaining on-task, and switching to a new task.

- If your child's disability includes social skills, as is true for children with a diagnosis on the autism spectrum, she may have trouble behaving appropriately with peers, making friends, understanding other people's points of view, and feeling empathy for others.

- If your child's disability includes difficulties and challenges with self-care/independent living skills, she may have challenges with daily tasks such as feeding, toileting, brushing teeth, bathing, dressing, using deodorant, and for more developmentally advanced individuals, tasks such as cooking, cleaning, and shopping.

In order to assess your child's abilities in different areas, it is important to know that his or her hearing and vision are adequate, or have been corrected, and that assessment of these areas is current. Talk to your child's teacher/therapists/school psychologist about your child's abilities in each area, to get age levels, and more understanding.

Vision and hearing

My child's vision was tested on (date):
Result:

My child's hearing was tested on (date):
Result:

Speech and language skills

My child makes the following speech errors (speak to your child's speech/language therapist):

In the area of speech/language, my child understands language at about a _____ -year-old level.

My child expresses language at about a _____-year-old level.

The average length of an utterance from my child is _____ words.

This means that my typical utterance to my child should be no more than _____words in length (twice the length of child's typical utterance).

Does my child understand word order in three-word statements (e.g., Sally tapped Sammy vs. Sammy tapped Sally)?

My child understands the following prepositions:
- ☐ in
- ☐ on
- ☐ under
- ☐ over
- ☐ between
- ☐ behind
- ☐ in front of

Does my child use both "yes" and "no"?

Does my child understand both "yes" and "no"?

(How do I know?)

Does my child understand "if-then" statements?

(You may want to talk to your child's speech/language therapist about whether your child understands if-then statements. If-then statements often have an implied "then" with the "then" not actually stated. But the statement may still be just as abstract. A clue that your child doesn't understand if-then statements is that he doesn't pay any attention when you say things like "if you don't stop throwing your toys we're not going to go to the park" or "if you finish your work you can have some ice cream."

Try statements like "no throwing," or show him a cookie and say "do your work," directing him back to his work with gestures when he tries to grab it. At first you may need to require just a small piece of work in return for a small piece of the cookie until he gets the idea. Or use a picture schedule showing him doing what you expect, and then getting the reward. Even this may be too abstract for some children, but it may help those who may have stronger visual skills than language skills. If these kinds of strategies work better than if-then statements, it may be an indication that he doesn't understand if-then statements.)

Fine motor skills

In the area of fine motor skills, my child functions at about a _____- year-old level.

The tasks my child finds challenging are:
- ☐ buttoning
- ☐ zipping/snapping
- ☐ using a fork
- ☐ spreading/cutting with a knife
- ☐ using a spoon
- ☐ writing/using a keyboard for typing
- ☐ turning on switches
- ☐ manipulating puzzle pieces
- ☐ building with blocks
- ☐ moving toy cars around

Visual-motor skills

In the area of visual-motor skills, my child's development is at about a _____-year-old level. (Ask your child's occupational therapist if this has been evaluated.)

My child has challenges with:

- ☐ copying shapes
- ☐ copying letters
- ☐ kicking a ball
- ☐ catching a ball
- ☐ hitting back a ball in volleyball

Gross motor skills

In the area of gross motor skills, my child's development is at about a _____-year-old level.

The activities my child finds challenging are:

- ☐ walking
- ☐ running
- ☐ jumping
- ☐ balancing
- ☐ understanding where his body is in space (e.g., bumps into people and things)
- ☐ learning a new skill or routine

Cognitive skills

In the area of cognitive development, my child is at about a _____-year-old level, with a verbal IQ of _____ and a nonverbal IQ of _____.

Does my child have difficulty applying learned skills in a new situation?

My child has an understanding of the following time concepts:

- ☐ later
- ☐ now
- ☐ wait
- ☐ first
- ☐ last
- ☐ next
- ☐ before
- ☐ after

Does my child understand same/different?

How long can my child remember something?

Does my child know where favorite foods or toys are kept?

Does my child make the connection between his good behavior and the reward, if you delay a reward for doing something well longer than an instant? (If you're not sure, then the answer may be "no".)

Attention

In the area of attention, you may not have an evaluation with an age-equivalence score, but it may help to think about children of different ages and how your child's attention span compares to them.

In the area of attention, my child seems like a _____-year-old child.

Does my child have difficulty staying with an activity?

The longest time my child can maintain attention is

_____.

My child has a longer attention span for the following kinds of activities (think about, e.g., school work vs. games, active vs. passive, visual vs. auditory kinds of activities, etc.):

My child has a shorter attention span for the following kinds of activities (think about the same kinds of things as above):

Social skills

In the area of social skills, my child is at about a _____-year-old level. The child may have been evaluated using the social domain of the Vineland Adaptive Behavior Scales, or some other instrument, and you have an age equivalence. There are also checklists available in many of the books listed in Appendix 2 (e.g., *Do-Watch-Listen-Say*, or the Skillstreaming series).

Does my child have *appropriate* ways to ask for attention?

Does my child know how to invite another to play on the playground?

Does my child know how to join others at play?

Does my child know how to initiate a conversation?

Does my child know how to join a conversation?

Does my child know how to express his feelings appropriately for his developmental level?

Does my child want to share experiences, feelings, toys?

Self-care/independent living skills

In the area of self-care/independent living skills, my child is at about a _____-year-old level. (You may have this information from the Vineland Adaptive Behavior Scales or other instruments.)

Does my child have challenges with dressing?

Does my child have challenges with feeding herself?

Does my child have challenges with toileting?

Does my child have challenges with brushing teeth?

Does my child have challenges with bathing?

Does my child have challenges with grooming?

Leisure skills

Does my child have difficulty knowing how to occupy himself or herself during leisure time?

Does my child have difficulty knowing how to begin an activity?

Implications of your child's abilities

Speech and language skills

Ways I can help my child understand what I say
For example:

- make sure you have your child's attention before speaking

- speak slowly

- speak very clearly, with appropriate intonation (sometimes exaggerated intonation helps gain the child's attention)

- use shorter phrases (no more than twice the average length of phrase the child uses)

- use pictures to illustrate what you are saying

- use gestures to reinforce what you are saying

- ask your child's speech/language therapist for more ideas.

Ways I can help my child express himself

For example:

- let him choose from several pictures to show an activity he wants to do

- let him choose from several objects to show what he wants

- teach him ways to indicate pain and discomfort (e.g., pointing to a picture of a grimace face when he is in pain, so that he can eventually tell you when he has pain)

- ask your child's speech/language therapist for more ideas.

Fine motor skills

Fine motor tasks and/or self-care tasks that are most challenging for my child right now:

Ways I could support my child to succeed at some part of these tasks

For example:

- demonstrating what to do

- starting it for the child

- doing all but the last step

- providing a visual cue after every step

- rewarding each step

- giving hand-over-hand assistance

- finding an easier but related task

- using adaptive equipment, e.g., for holding a spoon, gripping a pencil, etc. (ask your child's occupational therapist for more ideas)

- using picture schedules of the steps involved.

Gross motor skills

Gross motor activities that are most challenging for my child right now:

Ways I could support my child to succeed at some part of these activities (ask your child's physical therapist for ideas):

Cognitive skills

Ways I can help my child generalize skills:

- e.g. teach the concept of "same" with various materials and tasks, such as sorting, matching, and labeling as same or different

What is the longest I can wait before giving a reward or praise before things start to fall apart? (This may vary in different situations and activities, so make a note of that, too.)

- ☐ 30 seconds
- ☐ 1 minute
- ☐ 2 minutes
- ☐ 5 minutes
- ☐ 10 minutes

Attention

Ways I can support my child in developing her attention span, for example by not expecting too much, i.e., for some tasks it may be harder than others for your child to pay attention, so expect an attention span that is within what your child can do:

- Break tasks into small parts and only expect a little at a time.

- Provide breaks before attention runs out.

- Praise and reward for paying attention.

- Set a timer and tell her to stay on-task until it goes off.

- Have a series of pictures of the steps in the task.

- Use visual cues to remind your child to keep on-task.

Ways I can support my child in developing social skills

Probably one of the best ways is to advocate for your child to have have his social skills evaluated and to have social skills goals in his individual education plan (IEP) – the goals should be linked to a social skills curriculum – a "social skills group" or "friendship group" without clear and specific goals may not be much help.

Social skills

Ways I can support my child to ask for attention appropriately
For example help him to:

- initiate a fun routine/game

- say my name

- bring me a game

- give me a hug.

Ways I can support my child initiating appropriate activities:

- teach play routines (described on pages 78–79)

PART III

TARGET AND DEFINE BEHAVIOR

6

Go through a Typical Day

The first step in dealing with your child's behavior is to begin noticing the situations in which behavior is problematic, and begin prioritizing your concerns, so that you can start addressing them. You can't do everything at once! Let's start by going through a typical day. As you do so, notice:

- trouble spots/problem behaviors
- activities and objects your child dislikes
- positive, appropriate behaviors
- activities and objects your child enjoys
- whether you have some time for yourself.

Begin with when your child wakes up.

- Does he wake up before the rest of the family or do you have to drag him out of bed?
- How is the morning routine, and getting to school or the school bus?
- What kind of behaviors does school communicate about with you?
- What about daycare, if your child goes there before or after school?
- What is the afternoon like?
- Does your child want a snack?
- Is he tired or frustrated?
- Has he had a long bus ride?
- Are siblings around?

- When do the adults in your house get home?

- What are mealtimes like?

- Does your child entertain himself independently?

- What is bathtime like?

- What is bedtime like?

- Is there a bedtime routine?

- Does your child fall asleep easily?

- Does your child stay asleep?

Identify all the troubling behaviors and then start to prioritize. Identify the most troubling behavior. Sometimes working on one behavior helps you understand the dynamics of other difficult behaviors as well. But focus on one behavior to start with. Later, you'll develop a plan for that behavior. After you've done that, you can come back and work on other behaviors and develop plans for them as well. Identify all the positive behaviors as well, although the troubling behaviors may be easier to identify! Some examples of positive behaviors might be:

- occupies herself independently for one minute at a time

- waits for 30 seconds when told to "wait"

- shows interest in new materials

- plays catch with her brother when given a ball and some supervision

- responds well to praise (or sweets or whatever reward works)

- enjoys finishing a task.

Identifying positive behaviors will help you notice them so that you can reward them and make them more likely to increase. The more time your child is spending in positive behavior, the less time he or she will have for negative behavior. In other words, the more positive behaviors there are to compete with the negative ones, the less time your child will spend engaging in the negative behaviors.

Going through my day

Put an "x" in the box for the trouble spots.

- ☐ Waking up
- ☐ Toileting
- ☐ Getting dressed
- ☐ Grooming
- ☐ Eating breakfast
- ☐ Waiting for bus
- ☐ Getting on bus
- ☐ Riding on bus
- ☐ Getting off bus (when returning home)
- ☐ Arriving home
- ☐ Putting coat away
- ☐ Putting school things away
- ☐ Free time before dinner
- ☐ Homework
- ☐ Dinner time
- ☐ Playing after dinner
- ☐ Bathtime
- ☐ Bedtime routine
- ☐ Falling asleep
- ☐ Staying asleep

Behaviors at other times (may not be daily events)

- ☐ Getting in car (e.g., for errands, appointments)
- ☐ Wearing seat belt
- ☐ Riding in car
- ☐ Restaurants
- ☐ Grocery store

- ☐ Shopping
- ☐ Other stores
- ☐ Haircuts
- ☐ Waiting rooms (for doctor/dentist)
- ☐ Seeing the doctor/dentist
- ☐ Having company over
- ☐ Going to friends' houses
- ☐ Going to a park or playground
- ☐ Being with siblings

My child's behaviors

The troubling behaviors that my child engages in are (list as many as you can):

The positive and appropriate behaviors my child has are (list as many as you can):

The things my child dislikes or seems to be afraid of are:

The activities, toys, etc. that my child enjoys are (you can copy this from an earlier page):

The following are times each day or week that I have to myself:

(If you don't have anything to write here, be careful! It means you need to develop your support network. Go back and look at section 3 again.)

7

Define the Behavior

Now that you've identified troubling behaviors your child has, let's talk a bit more about how to define these behaviors. The important points of a good definition of behavior are that it be objective, and measurable, with the following aspects covered: duration, intensity, frequency.

For example, you may say that your child "tantrums" when she does not get her way. Children tantrum in different ways. A more precise way of stating it would be that she yells, kicks, and hits people in her vicinity, for up to 30 minutes, that she hits and kicks hard enough to cause bruising, and yells loud enough to be heard next door, and that this happens at least twice a day.

Note that the behavior is objectively described: yelling, kicking, and hitting. Also note that duration (30 minutes) is included; intensity (kicks and hits hard enough to cause bruising, and yells loud enough to be heard next door) is included; and frequency (this happens at least twice a day) is also included. With this kind of description you could measure the behavior, and see changes in it. For example, you would have some basis for measuring whether the tantrums were decreasing in intensity, duration, or frequency.

Defining behavior

In the following fictitious examples, make up a measurable definition of the behavior that is mentioned. Remember to include an objective description, and information about intensity, duration, and frequency. Information on what generally occurs just before the behavior begins is also useful, if known (sample answers on page 58).

Defining behavior

Jerry is verbally abusive

Jane has no self-control

Sally is non-compliant

Defining behavior

Jerry is verbally abusive

Jerry talks to adults using phrases such as "you're stupid," "I don't like you," and "you're ugly," two to three times per day, usually when told he can't have something he wants. Jerry usually intensifies the loudness of these statements until he is screaming loudly enough to hurt the ears of anyone else in the room, and then he begins kicking and hitting. He usually does not settle down until after he has been put in time-out, and the entire episode can last up to 20 minutes.

Jane has no self-control

Whenever Jane has to wait, e.g., for lunch, before riding in the car to go to the park, etc., she starts whimpering, lying on the floor, thrashing, and kicking. If anyone is in her vicinity when she is kicking, she can kick hard enough to cause tissue damage. This can continue until whatever she is waiting for is provided. On occasion, it has continued up to 45 minutes, although she does not usually have to wait this long. This occurs at least once a day, and usually occurs three to four times per day.

Sally is non-compliant

When Sally is given two- or three-step directions, she does not follow more than the first step, almost 100 percent of the time. If given only one-step directions, she follows them nearly every time. This response occurs whenever she is given directions, at least seven to eight times per day.

8

Agree on a Prioritized List of Troubling Behaviors

If you have a spouse or other person(s) closely involved with your child, do you agree about what behaviors are troubling? Do you agree about which is the most troubling? If not, you will have to come to an agreement about what is most troubling. It may help to clearly and objectively define each behavior, as described above. Even if there is no one else other than you who is closely involved with the child, clearly and objectively defining each behavior will help you to be sure you have the list prioritized correctly.

Now go through the lists you made earlier of troubling/undesirable behaviors and positive behaviors, and rewrite them, if necessary, so they are objectively described, and include intensity, duration, and frequency information.

Troubling behavior

Undesirable behaviors
(objective description):   intensity   duration   frequency

Positive behaviors:

What is *the most* troubling behavior at this time that you and another significant person involved with the child (if there is one) would agree on?

Prioritize the rest of the list. Go through and number the other troubling behaviors in order according to how troubling each one is.

PART IV

FUNCTIONS OF BEHAVIOR

9

Common Functions of Behavior and How to Address Them

In the next few pages we will be looking at some of the common functions of challenging behaviors. It is important to understand what function the behavior serves for your child in order to transform it into something more positive. This is what's involved in a "functional behavior assessment," a term you may have heard. The same behavior can serve different functions for different people. For example, one child might scream because she likes the sound. Another child might scream because she likes the attention that results from the screaming. Another child might scream to express frustration at what is being asked of her, with no interest in the resulting sound or attention. A child might scream for all of those reasons at different times. Some common functions of behavior are listed below. Keep in mind that these functions may overlap.

- Discomfort – medical or environmental.

- Developmental levels (expectations are either too high or too low).

- Seeking rewards – in general this is usually involved.

- Escape/avoidance of a task.

- Seeking sensory stimulation, e.g., likes the sight of spinning objects or the feel of water.

- Avoiding sensory stimulation, e.g., dislikes certain sounds, or the feel of tags on shirts.

- Difficulty with organization needed to initiate an appropriate activity.

- Attention seeking/wanting to interact and not knowing how to initiate an interaction appropriately.

- Expressing frustration/anger.

- Expressing fear.

- Difficulty waiting.

- Expressing "Wait! Let me finish!"

- Expressing "No!"

- Other communication.

Discomfort – medical or environmental

You may recognize the medical list below from the beginning of this workbook.

Medical

Pain/discomfort

    Dental

    Gastrointestinal (stomach ache, reflux, ulcer, etc.)

    Joints/muscles

    Headache

    Ears

    Eyes

    Lungs

    Menstrual

    Other gynecological

    Other

Allergies

Medication side effects (specify)

Hunger

Thirst

Tiredness

Illness (cold, stomach flu, etc.)

Environmental

Clothing too tight

Tags irritating the skin (shirt tags may need to be cut off)

Fabric feels unpleasant to child

Room

Too hot

Too cold

Too noisy

Too light

Fluorescent lighting

Dark/dim

Unpleasant smells

Noises in the environment

Outside noises such as lawn mowers, garbage trucks, sirens

Inside noises such as vacuum, washer, furnace, airconditioner, fan

Not enough personal space, child or belongings are crowded

When the behavior occurs, run through these lists and start noticing whether these factors are present. See your child's doctor and/or modify the environment as appropriate.

Developmental levels – expectations may be too high

Look at the behavior in terms of the task demands; in other words, what skills must the child have to successfully perform this task? For purposes of discussion a "task" can be anything, even occupying oneself during leisure time can be considered a "task." When you look at task demands, you consider what the requirements are in terms of language, motor skills, cognitive skills, attention and organizational skills, social skills, and daily living skills.

For example, if your child is dawdling while getting dressed, and has a tantrum when you try to urge him to hurry, think about the task demands, i.e., what is required to succeed at the task:

- Does he understand the language you use when you tell him to get dressed, or to put on pants before shoes?

- Does he have the fine motor skill to move his fingers in such a way that he can button, and otherwise manipulate the clothing to get dressed?

- Does he have the spatial skills to understand how to orient his clothing so that it goes on the right way?

- Does he have the cognitive skills to remember how to do things and to remember all he has to do and in what sequence to do it correctly?

- Does he have the social awareness and maturity to care whether he is dressed properly or not?

- Does he have the ability to screen out sensory stimulation that bothers him (e.g., the feeling of the clothing or tags) or in the environment that distracts him from the task?

Another example would be that your child gets into things in the evenings and makes a mess. What are the task demands? Your child must be able to initiate an appropriate leisure activity, stay with it, and then select another appropriate activity if he gets tired of doing that activity. The task demands are high. The child must have skills to perform a leisure activity such as doing a puzzle, reading a book, watching and understanding the plot of a cartoon or other TV show. Then he must have the skills to stay with it, realize he is bored, put the first activity away and make another choice.

Another example would be getting ready for bed. You tell your child she must go to bed in a half-hour so she needs to start getting ready for bed now. The task demands are that your child have a conceptual understanding of time, in general, and specifically how much time a half-hour is, how long it takes to perform certain activities, and how long that time is in comparison to a half-hour. She must understand the language you use to tell her all this, and must have the organizational and motor skills to perform the required actions in the correct order. She must have the ability to filter out distracting stimulation and to cope with the sensory qualities of her nightgown, bedclothes, and bedroom (e.g., ticking clock, too much light).

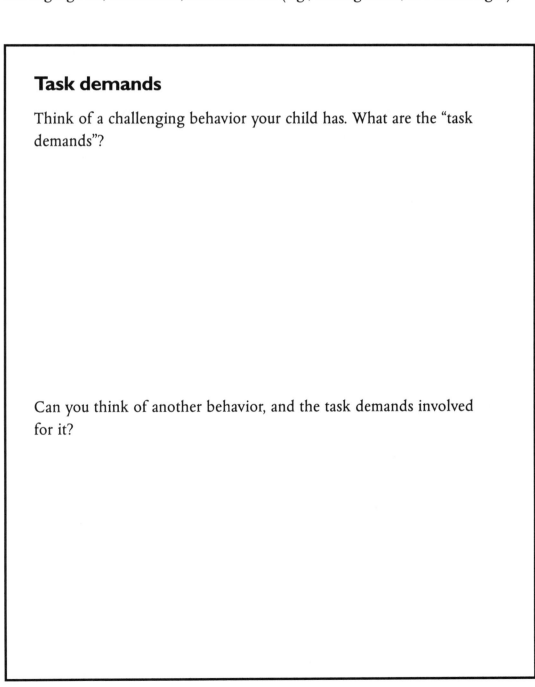

Task demands

Think of a challenging behavior your child has. What are the "task demands"?

Can you think of another behavior, and the task demands involved for it?

Seeking rewards

At some level, the behavior of each of us is aimed at getting more rewards. That's why it's very important that you use rewards in order to motivate positive behavior in your child. For some of us it may be the reward of a paycheck. For some, it may be the more sophisticated rewards of doing a job well, or seeing someone else happy. But it is about rewards. We don't engage in an activity hoping it will lead to unhappiness.

Your child may be misbehaving to get the rewards of increased attention. Even negative attention can be rewarding, especially if the child is not getting much attention. For children who seem oblivious to attention, it may be the reward of creating a noisy, interesting spectacle, which occurs in reaction to their misbehavior.

What is a reward?

A reward is anything that tends to increase the behavior that precedes it. Nothing is intrinsically a reward. A reward is only a reward if it increases the preceding behavior. Rewards are not limited to sweets or other small treats. A reward can be praise, acknowledgment, an object, an activity, an interaction, a physical sensation, listening to music, etc. (See the Reward/Reinforcer Survey in Appendix 1.)

Some people say that "rewards don't work" with their child. Rewards work, by definition. What they mean is that they have not yet found what is rewarding for their child, and/or they are using the rewards too infrequently and/or too late (too long after the positive behavior occurred) to function as a reward. In other words, a child may work for a cookie, but she might not work for a cookie crumb. Or, a child might work for the opportunity to play a favorite game with their caregiver for 20 minutes, but they might not work for the opportunity to play for five seconds.

The importance of rewards

Just as it is critical to identify positive behaviors, it is critical to build those positive behaviors by rewarding them.

Use rewards frequently and immediately

You should be using rewards, such as praise, at least five times as often as you use reprimands. For many children with special needs, waiting until the end of an afternoon, or even waiting until the end of an hour, may be too long for the child to make the connection between the reward and why they got the reward. Also, it may be too infrequent to motivate the child. If you're not sure, it's better to err on the side of giving the reward more immediately and more often. For example, one little boy was getting a very positive reward program at school, with stickers and treats at the end of every class period for appropriate behavior. The system was not working at all, but when his teachers began rewarding him immediately after a positive behavior, throughout each class period, his behavior improved dramatically.

Make explicit what you are rewarding

The other thing the teachers in the above example did to make their program successful was to highlight for the child the positive behaviors they wanted to see increase. Out of all the possible positive behaviors they wanted to see, they chose three that were their highest priority. His verbal skills were quite limited, so they constructed picture cards, with illustrations of each of the three behaviors. When they "caught" him engaging in the good behaviors, they used a verbal comment ("nice sitting") paired with showing him the picture, as they gave him the reward.

Rewards are not bribes!

Some people feel that using rewards to motivate positive behaviors is bribing their child and that it is not a good idea. There is an important difference, however, between a reward and a bribe. The connotation often associated with a "bribe" is that it is something used to motivate a negative behavior of some kind: doing something illegal, unethical, and/or harmful to other people. Using rewards to motivate your child's positive behavior is not the same thing at all! Your child will be doing something that will be good for him or her, and for those around him or her, as well. Although we may not usually think of it this way, it's normal for all of us to get rewards for appropriate behavior. For example, we get rewarded for our thoughtfulness with appreciation from a friend or spouse, and as mentioned above, we get rewarded for doing our job with a paycheck.

External rewards vs. internal motivation

Of course it would be wonderful if everyone did the right thing because they want to do it, with no external rewards needed. But if your child never learns what it is like to behave positively, how can she ever learn about the intrinsic rewards of those behaviors? Until she learns that, supporting her with extrinsic rewards (food, toys, privileges, etc.) can help shape those behaviors; this can eventually lead to more internally motivated behavior.

Using self-stimulating activities as rewards

If a child has a particular object or activity that he uses for self-stimulation, e.g., waving a stick in front of his face, people sometimes are reluctant to use that object or activity as a reward. Even though the child clearly enjoys the "stimming," people may feel that the behavior is undesirable and should be eliminated, rather than encourage it by using it as a reward.

Another way to look at this is that the behavior can be a very powerful motivator. The behavior is important to the child for some reason and it doesn't seem ethical or even possible to completely eliminate the behavior (assuming it is not causing injury to the child or others, of course). Limiting the behavior rather than trying to eradicate it may be a more reasonable approach. Often you can use the behavior to encourage positive behaviors. For example, one girl with Rett's syndrome was encouraged to engage in more instrumental behaviors with her hands by being rewarded with a mirror, which she loved to look into. Another example is that several programs for teaching pretend play to children with autism use the child's favorite "stim" objects as rewards for engaging in tasks that promote the development of pretend play.

Appropriate expectations

No matter how well you use rewards, if the expectations are beyond the child's level, you will not succeed. That is why section 5, page 35 on expectations is critical.

Reward menu

It is important to have a "menu" of rewards, so that one reward doesn't become stale and ineffective. Keep rotating the rewards so they stay fresh and motivating. You can also give your child choices among two or three possible rewards. See the Reward/Reinforcer Survey in Appendix 1 for ideas that will help you generate a menu of rewards for your child. After you have looked over the survey, answer the following questions:

Develop a reward menu

Does my child enjoy attention?

Does my child enjoy praise?

Does my child enjoy applause?

What objects does my child show interest in?

What activities does my child enjoy?

What music does my child like?

What sensations does my child like (e.g., bouncing, swinging, riding in a car, being rubbed, the feel of sand, water, textures such as velvet)?

Does my child require immediate, easily-delivered rewards, such as stickers, sweets, praise, a back rub, etc.?

Can my child work for a period of time before getting the reward?

How long can my child behave well before getting the reward (based on your own experience)?

After looking at the reward survey in Appendix 1 and answering the above questions about rewards, list below the items/activities that will be on your child's reward menu. Be sure to include plenty of easily-dispensed rewards that you can give immediately.

Reward menu

Escape/avoidance of a task

Challenging behaviors often occur as a way of avoiding or escaping unpleasant, or not sufficiently pleasant, situations. Avoidance occurs before the task or situation has started, so that the child can avoid engaging in it at all. Escape occurs after the activity has started and the child escapes having to continue with it.

Sufficiently disruptive behaviors can lead to removal from the situation, and some children appear able to make this connection and use it to their advantage. The child may engage in other activities that are more interesting to him or her, to make the situation more bearable. These behaviors may be undesirable from an adult perspective, but serve the child by allowing him or her to escape the demands of the situation. Another possibility is that the child may shut down and not become involved in the activity, avoiding or escaping through passivity.

We all do this. If we are involved in an activity that is too frustrating, or not sufficiently rewarding, we try to escape. As adults we understand the unwritten rules of society, and we are able to show some restraint, rather than throwing things, hitting people, or running out of the room. We may, however, covertly try to do something else so people won't notice, e.g., day-dreaming during a boring meeting. We may also engage in another activity to make the situation more palatable. For example, we may talk to someone while standing in line at the grocery store because we are tired of just standing and waiting. We may postpone something we don't want to do as long as we can possibly get away with it (e.g., getting an extension to do our taxes). These are just a few examples.

Task avoidance

Some situations or tasks that my child may be seeking to avoid or to escape are:

Some possible reasons why my child seeks to avoid/escape are (list reasons for each situation above):

Understanding why your child is frustrated can lead you to make positive changes

It becomes important to understand what it is about a situation or activity that is frustrating for the child. There may be environmental factors, task demands that are beyond the child's developmental level, sensory issues (e.g., sounds or sights that bother her or that she is drawn to and distract her), insufficient frequency of rewards, etc. In other words, the various topics discussed in this workbook will become relevant in understanding why the child tries to avoid or escape certain situations.

Once you understand why your child is frustrated, you can begin to look at ways to modify the situation or expectations to make it more agreeable to your child.

Seeking sensory stimulation

Some children may engage in challenging behaviors in order to seek sensory stimulation. This is often the case for children with a diagnosis on the autism spectrum. They may seem to require more sensory input than is typical. This can apply to each of the senses:

- visual

- auditory

- olfactory (smell)

- tactile (touch)

- gustatory (taste)

- kinesthetic (receptors in joints, muscles, tendons and ligaments stimulated by bodily movements and tensions).

For example, they may:

- bounce or spin themselves for the kinesthetic stimulation

- rub things on their faces for the tactile stimulation, or may play in water because of the way it feels

- like the feeling of being in small spaces or to be wrapped up in a towel or sheet

- make noises or be drawn to certain kinds of sounds or music, for the auditory stimulation

- seek out certain sights, such as spinning objects, or shiny things, for the visual stimulation
- like to smell people's hair or smell objects, because they enjoy the smell.

The trick is to find socially acceptable and safe ways for the child to find the desired sensory stimulation. Below are some acceptable sensory equivalents for common unacceptable sensory stimulation. Beneath the undesirable behavior suggested substitutes are listed. Try redirecting to the acceptable substitute.

Playing with own or someone else's hair

Substitute the:

- silky fringe on pillow
- yarn doll
- doll with hair.

Playing with water

(The substitute may depend on which sensory qualities the child is seeking.)

- Confine the water play to bath or wading pool.
- Use a box of beans that can be poured and may share some of the visual properties of water.
- Provide a motion/lava lamp, which may share some of the visual qualities of water movement.
- Provide hand cream, which feels cool and wet like water.

Turning on switches, unlocking locks

- Mount some hardware on a board and let the child play with that (e.g., locks, bolts, switches).
- Find a toy that has parts with latches and other things that can be opened and closed, such as doll furniture.

Pushing another child

Push a Bobo doll (large inflatable figure with weighted base, so it pops up when pushed).

Throwing things

Toss a foam, rubber or other lightweight ball into a box in one particular corner of a particular room.

Playing with window blind cords

Provide a *short* piece of ribbon (not long enough to wrap around neck and choke on).

Attraction to fire

- Watch video of a Yule log.

- Watch a motion/lava lamp.

- Provide rainsticks (some are clear plastic with beads inside that fall).

Putting things in mouth

Chewing on plastic tubing (ask an occupational therapist).

Wanting to ride in the car all the time

Sitting on top of a running washing machine or dryer may vibrate in a similar manner (but will need supervision); sitting and leaning against it may work also.

Playing with feces

Use play dough; there are also home-made play dough recipes that you can make with various scents.

Smearing food

- a koosh ball

- play dough

Avoiding sensory stimulation

This was covered earlier under "medical/environmental" factors. Your child may be especially sensitive and react negatively to certain sounds, smells, tastes, textures, sights, kinds of movement, positions, etc.

Which of these sensory stimuli is my child sensitive to?

Sounds

- ☐ Sirens
- ☐ Vacuum cleaner
- ☐ Washing machine
- ☐ Animal sounds
- ☐ Fan
- ☐ Heating system
- ☐ Fireworks
- ☐ Certain kinds of music
- ☐ The sound of nylon clothes (e.g., pant legs rubbing against each other)
- ☐ Other (specify)…

Sights

- ☐ Bright lights
- ☐ Fluorescent lights
- ☐ Cars going by
- ☐ TV
- ☐ Other (specify)…

Smells

- ☐ Foods
- ☐ Animal (specify dog, cat, etc.)
- ☐ Soaps and detergents
- ☐ Markers
- ☐ Glue
- ☐ Perfume
- ☐ Candles
- ☐ Restaurants
- ☐ Other (specify)…

Tastes

- ☐ Certain foods
- ☐ Other (specify)…

Textures

- ☐ Tags on undershirts or shirts
- ☐ Plastic
- ☐ Wool clothes
- ☐ Nylon clothes
- ☐ Certain upholstery fabric
- ☐ Other (specify)…

Kinds of movement or positions

- ☐ Being seated or on playground equipment with feet not touching the floor
- ☐ Being picked up
- ☐ Swinging
- ☐ Riding in car
- ☐ Riding in wagon
- ☐ Other (specify)…

Difficulty with organization needed to initiate an appropriate activity

Children often get into trouble when they can't organize themselves to do something more appropriate. This can cause problems.

Develop independent play routines

The more options your child has for appropriately occupying himself, the less likely he will be to get into trouble. Put together a box of activities he can do and teach him a routine of playing with each, one at a time, and afterwards putting it in another box (the "finished" box). This is a strategy used at the TEACCH program in North Carolina, USA.

Some things that might be good are puzzles, pegs, and picture books. Start with only one or two.

If he enjoys looking at pictures, you might want to make some books of favorite photos, or make a book of pictures of him going to the park, or the zoo, or other activity of interest to him, and make a book for each of these outings. He may enjoy looking at something personally meaningful, and may stay with it longer than another book. Reward him for following this routine.

Develop positive play routines for your child and his sibling(s)

If your child's sibling is playing at a more advanced level than he is, it may be disruptive for him to be included in his sibling's play; however, his sibling may find it rewarding to help him to learn some of the play activities described above in the section on independent play routines. See the section at the end of this workbook on peer interaction games, page 129.

Picture schedules

If your child has good visual skills, you might want to capitalize on these skills by creating a picture schedule for the afternoon play routine, or evening, or both. For example, you could have a picture of him and his sibling playing, to represent some play time with his sibling; then a picture of the toy box and "finished" box to represent him playing alone; then a picture of a TV to represent watching a video; then dinner time, etc. You can use a poster with velcro to mount the pictures representing the schedule for the day. You can take off each picture as you finish that segment of the schedule. Or you can have the pictures mounted on tagboard covered with clear contact, and use a washable marker to place a checkmark or tick below each picture when it is completed.

Attention seeking/wanting to interact and not knowing how to initiate appropriately

Challenging behaviors are often due to a desire for attention/interaction, but the child may not have the skills to seek this appropriately. For example, the child may hit, kick, pinch, or bite because this is a sure-fire way to get a response from the other person. Or the child may yell, climb on the furniture, or run out the door, because this, too, is sure to bring a response. This is not to deny that the child may do these things for other reasons, as well, but the need for attention is a basic need, even in children with autism who appear to be oblivious to other people. In children with autism, the child may experience attention differently in some cases, i.e., the child observes a reaction rather than has a sense of another person attending to him, but it is still attention.

Children need ways to communicate greetings, as well as to communicate bids to play together or to receive attention, whether they can speak or not. Children who are nonverbal can be given pictures (of a social activity) that they can point to, they can learn to give high-fives, or they can learn to bring a favorite toy to someone to indicate they want to play together (e.g., a ball for playing catch). If they have some language skills they can be taught to say "play with me," "read story," "rub my back," etc.

It's important for all children that they get attention *before* they are tempted to ask for it in negative ways. This means that they get plenty of attention when they are being good, and plenty of attention all day, every day.

Attention seeking

When does my child currently get attention? (List times of day, and behaviors, negative or positive, that get attention):

The ways in which my child is able to ask for attention are (see above, e.g., pictures, short phrases, gestures, bringing objects):

The ways my child could learn to ask for attention are (consider whether your child is verbal or not and use the strategies above as appropriate):

Expressing frustration/anger

Aggression is a serious behavior because of the harm it can do others as well as the harm it may do the child who shows aggression (by limiting access to various opportunities, as a result of the behavior).

Check out medical and dental issues

Children can be more irritable and prone to aggression if they are ill, or have a headache or other discomfort. Make sure the child has had routine physicals and follow-up regarding any concerns. Make sure the child has routine dental exams and follow-up regarding any concerns. For some children, this may mean finding a doctor and/or dentist who is experienced in working with children with special needs. See earlier sections on medical factors and Appendix 2 for some resources.

Check out environmental factors

Children can be more irritable and prone to aggression if they are uncomfortable due to environmental factors. Some children are much more sensitive than the typical child. Consider factors such as temperature, noise level, harsh/bright lighting, odors, and textures of furniture upholstery and clothing (e.g., some children are bothered by tags on shirts).

Look for patterns

Does the behavior tend to occur with certain people, at certain times, in response to certain kinds of events? Look for patterns and determine whether there are any environmental manipulations you can make that might decrease the behavior.

Label the behavior

Make the behavior salient to the child by labeling it with as few words as possible when it occurs, e.g., *"No hitting!" "No pinching!" "No pushing!"* etc., so that the label for the action stands out clearly. If you say, "You know you're not supposed to hit; how would you like it if someone did that to you; that hurts, you know…" then the word "hit" is nearly drowned in a sea of words.

Label the emotion

If the child is angry, also label the emotion, with as few words as possible, e.g., "You're mad!" (cross).

Set up clear consequences

Time-out is usually a last resort, but with behaviors that are dangerous to others it is important to stop the behavior immediately and keep others safe. Time-out, in conjunction with the suggestions below for teaching alternatives and positive behaviors, may be the best response. When you put the child in time-out, get his attention, say "no hitting!" (or whatever is appropriate to the behavior), but do not discuss it any further at that time. If the child is too combative to be placed in time-out, consider "reverse time-out" in which you, and any others present, leave the area. Find a location from which you can monitor the child without being seen, e.g., by looking through the crack of a door, standing hidden around the corner, or a piece of furniture. Use approximately one minute of time-out for every year of the child's *mental* age.

Follow through with consequences consistently

Be sure to follow through with the consequences immediately, every time the behavior occurs. If the child engages in the behavior in a milder form, it may still be important to follow through with the consequence. If you don't, you need to be sure that the child can distinguish hitting lightly from hitting hard. Many times, the child cannot make this distinction, and responding inconsistently will only confuse him.

Teach alternative behaviors

If the behavior was dangerous to the child or others and you used time-out, after you release the child from time-out direct him to an appropriate behavior, such as playing with a toy, playing catch with you, or other interaction. If the child's behavior is not severe enough to warrant time-out, go directly to redirection. Teach the child to say "I'm mad!" (cross) when he is upset, rather than hitting. Do this by intervening when the child is angry, by saying something like "Are you mad?! Say 'I'm mad!'" (Note: "mad" is chosen over "angry" because it is only one syllable. For many children, the shorter the word (even a difference of only one syllable), the more likely it is that they will use the word when they need it.)

Consider language development

Many children become angry and frustrated when they cannot communicate, either because they do not know how to express what they need to or because they have an idea of what they want to express but can't convey it so others can understand. Know the child's level of language development and work with the speech/language clinician to provide as much support as possible for the child to communicate (e.g., with pictures, and short phrases). Focus on *functional* communication so that the child can communicate about daily events: e.g., what he wants, how he is feeling, what he likes, what he does not like, what he is afraid of, what he needs help with, and when something hurts. For your child, there may be other important functions not listed here.

Teach understanding of emotions

Sometimes children are aggressive because they don't know how else to express anger and frustration. Teaching them to label emotions can be helpful. Use pictures of people with various facial expressions that they can label as "happy," "sad," "cross," and "scared." You can also work on this while watching movies on TV, or videos; when you see someone displaying one of those emotions, simply label it, with as few words as possible ("he's cross!"). You can label the child's own emotions as they occur. You can work in front of a mirror, making faces representing these emotions, and labeling them, always with as few words as possible.

Teach positive behaviors

Sometimes children are aggressive because they don't know how else to interact with someone, or how else to gain someone else's attention. Teach positive social behaviors such as greeting, showing something of interest, asking to join in a game, and participating appropriately in a game. See curricula such as the *Skillstreaming* series or *Do-Watch-Listen-Say* by Kathleen Ann Quill, or *Giggle Time* by Susan Aud Sonders (full details in Appendix 2) for specific lesson plans and ideas.

Reward positive behaviors

When your child is controlling himself, engaging in positive social behaviors, or labeling his emotions instead of being aggressive, be sure to reward profusely and frequently for these behaviors. Use praise and other rewards. The child should be getting at least five times as many rewards as reprimands and time-outs. Generate a reward menu so that you can rotate rewards to keep them effective. Some children respond well to a reward chart, with stickers, stars, or smiley faces for good behavior. Some children need something more concrete.

Give lots of attention

Often children are aggressive because they like what follows, such as attention. Even negative attention can be better than being ignored. Make sure the child gets plenty of adult attention and interaction and don't make him "ask" for attention by becoming aggressive.

Self-esteem

Self-esteem can be an underlying issue in angry and aggressive behavior. See the section on self-esteem, page 124.

Dealing with aggression

Some possible causes of my child's aggression are:

If the environment might be a cause of aggression, what are some ways I could modify the environment?

If seeking attention might be a cause of aggression, what are some ways I could give more attention?

If lack of understanding of emotions might be a cause of aggression, how could I teach understanding of emotions?

If challenges in communication might be a cause of aggression, what nonverbal means of communication could I help my child learn (pointing to pictures, handing you something he wants, clapping, etc.)?

How could I reward appropriate alternative behaviors to aggression?

Fighting with siblings

Sometimes the aggression may take the form of fighting with siblings. This occurs frequently enough that we will devote a whole section to this issue. A child may fight with her sibling for a number of reasons, e.g., not knowing more appropriate ways to interact with the sibling, wanting attention from the sibling, wanting attention from parents (which may result from fighting with the sibling), or not knowing how else to express being angry at the sibling for something the sibling does. Typically developing children may sometimes need time to be alone and become annoyed when not left alone by their sibling with a developmental disability. They may sometimes resent the extra attention that a child with special needs often requires, and they may express this resentment.

Talk to your child's sibling about it

If your child has a sibling who has been the target of his aggression, talk to the sibling about it. Allow the sibling to express how the behavior has affected him or her. Help him or her to understand the child's differences from typically developing children, why the child may behave aggressively, and what you are doing about it. Be alert for signs of damage to the sibling's self-esteem, or signs of frustration and resentment, and obtain counseling for the sibling if needed.

Teach and reward positive play routines

Teach and reward positive ways of interacting so that the child and her siblings will have positive alternatives to fighting. See the section on peer interaction games on page 129 for some ideas.

Protect the sibling's time, space, and belongings

Don't expect sibling(s) to be constantly available to the child with a developmental disability. Make sure that they have some privacy, i.e., somewhere they can retreat to and be undisturbed, and that their belongings are off-limits to their brother or sister with a developmental disability (although there may be other items that belong to both).

Make sure the sibling gets some of your attention

Make sure the sibling is getting attention in positive ways so that he or she does not have to resort to fighting with the brother or sister with a developmental disability to get your attention.

Fighting with siblings

Do/does my child's sibling(s) understand his or her special needs?

Are my child's sibling's time, space, and possessions protected?

What are some positive ways to reward my child's sibling for working with the rest of the family in promoting positive behavior in my child with special needs?

Do I find ways to give attention to my child's sibling and acknowledge the special stresses as well as the special opportunities of the situation for him or her?

Enlist cooperation of the sibling

After you make sure that the sibling's time, space, and possessions are protected, discuss the situation with him or her. If you would like the sibling to direct the child to "stop," instead of engaging in fighting, talk about why this is important, and the importance of saying "stop" consistently.

Teach the sibling how to deal with aggression

Teach the sibling to say "No!" when the child is aggressive, and to get adult help. Find ways to keep the sibling physically safe (e.g., keeping the children separated when an adult is not in the same room).

Talk about the sibling's feelings about their brother or sister with special needs

Discuss with the sibling how he or she feels about a child with special needs being part of the family. Explain how his brother or sister is different from typically developing children, and may need special help and extra time from parents. There are many resources available for siblings, e.g., books and websites (see Appendix 2).

Reward positive behavior

If the child and her sibling are playing well together, or if they are both at home and not playing together but *not* fighting, be sure to reward them both frequently and enthusiastically (every few minutes). Develop a menu of rewards for your child so that the rewards can be rotated. This keeps any one reward from becoming routine, and helps the rewards to remain effective.

Use sibling resources

See Appendix 2 for resources such as books, websites, and workshops for siblings. Your child's sibling does not have to feel alone!

Expressing fear

A child may engage in challenging behaviors due to fear. They may not know how to express their fears or seek comfort appropriately.

Identify the fearful stimulus

Children with developmental disabilities may develop unusual fears. They may fear things that most of us would never think of as fearful, and on the other hand, they may not fear things that should evoke fear. They may have a negative experience with a person, object, or activity on one occasion and develop an intense fear forever after. They may associate things in ways that we would not, so that something is feared because they associate it with something fearful. Their fears may be based on unusual sensory responses. For example, it is not unusual for children with autism to be afraid of things like vacuum cleaners and dishwashers, resulting from their sensory sensitivity to the sounds these devices make. They may be afraid if something familiar is different in some way. For example, some children have been afraid of their own parent when he or she is dressed in an engulfing parka, or wearing glasses that the child is not used to seeing him or her wear. Sometimes children are afraid when they don't know what to expect, so changes in routine and transitions may cause fear.

Pair the fearful stimulus with something more positive

Once you have identified the fearful stimulus, pair it with something more positive. This may mean introducing the feared stimulus for very brief periods, and at a distance, while engaging the child in some positive and fun activity or giving the child a treat of some kind (e.g., a favorite food) at the same time. This must be done so that the positive far outweighs the negative, otherwise the positive stimulus (fun activity or treat) may be "contaminated" by the negative, and take on negative properties for the child instead of the intended effect. For example, if your child is afraid of the sound of the dishwasher, turn it on when she is in a room far away, play some music to mask the sound, and give your child a treat, while it is on. Gradually you may be able to lower the volume of the masking music, and bring her closer to where the dishwasher is.

Provide advance notice of what to expect

Use picture schedules to help your child understand what is coming next.

Provide comfort

See the section on helping your child stay calm on page 126 for ideas on how to provide comfort during times when your child is afraid.

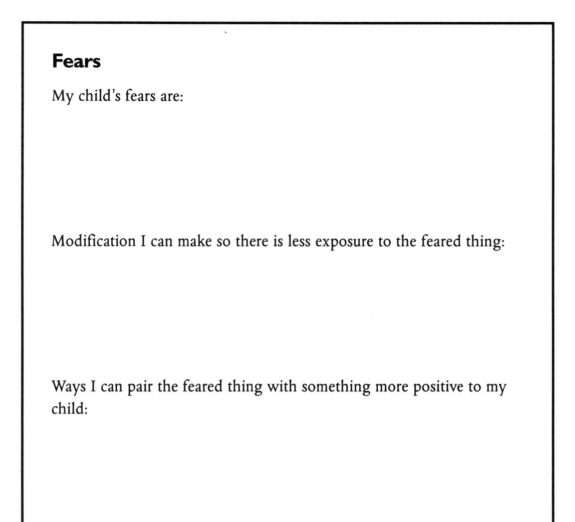

Fears

My child's fears are:

Modification I can make so there is less exposure to the feared thing:

Ways I can pair the feared thing with something more positive to my child:

Difficulty waiting

"Wait" is an important concept for children to learn in order to organize their behavior and learn more effectively, and also in order to get along with others.

Some children enjoy playing a waiting "game." This provides practice in learning to wait and makes it fun. You can have the child wait for a few seconds in any situation, e.g., before going outside, before throwing a ball, before answering how old he or she is, etc. If the child stops and waits while you count to three, or five (experiment to find a time interval that is challenging, but not too hard), then make a big fuss and say, "You waited!" Gradually increase the length of waiting required.

Once the idea becomes familiar, and he or she has positive associations to "waiting," then it may be easier to use the command to "wait" at stressful times when you need the child to wait. Don't expect results right away! You may have to practice for weeks or a few months before you start to see results.

You can also work on this while you are setting up materials or games for your child. Tell him or her to "wait," and then gently hold his or her hands down. Use just the one word, not a discussion of waiting and why it's important. After a moment or two, the child can be allowed to handle the materials. Repeat this process a number of times. After several times, say "wait," but hold the hands more lightly. Then say "wait," and touch the hands, but withdraw them right away. The idea is to help the child respond to the word "wait," by itself, by gradually fading other cues.

Another approach to waiting, which you may need to use before the above strategies start to have results, is to give the child something appropriate to do with his or her hands while waiting, e.g., something to hold, fold, and/or squeeze.

Expressing "Wait! Let me finish!"

Sometimes a child acts out because she doesn't know how to tell you to wait. It's really important to her to finish something. Particularly for children with a diagnosis on the autism spectrum, stopping before something is completed can be very upsetting. It's like listening to a tune with the last note or two left off. You want to hear those last notes. It's even more important to finish if the activity is ritualistic for the child. Children with a diagnosis on the autism spectrum often engage in ritualistic activities.

As was discussed in the section on "attention seeking," it's important for children, whether verbal or not, to have some way of communicating "Wait! Let me finish!" in an appropriate way. They can use a sign or picture, or just learn to say "Finish!" to communicate this.

You can use a timer to help them understand that they must finish in a certain length of time. Set the timer and tell her she will have to stop when the bell rings.

Expressing "No!"

Every child needs to have a way to say "No!" If they can't say it in words, they need to be able to hold up a picture, or make a sign or gesture.

Understanding the child's developmental level and sensory issues are important in understanding the kinds of things that the child will find intolerable. You might want to review those sections.

Other communication

Behavior in general is usually a form of communication. Some of the more common communication functions have been discussed, but be alert to other things that your child may be trying to communicate with behavior.

Strong dislikes

Things my child finds intolerable:

Ways I can find to make these situations/things occur less frequently, or to pair them with something positive, during or afterwards:

PART V

CREATE A BEHAVIOR PLAN

10

Antecedents and Consequences

Keep a log of the next five occurrences of the highest-priority troubling behavior, which you selected earlier, in section 8, page 60. Each time, answer the following questions related to antecedents (what occurred right before the behavior) and consequences (what occurred right after the behavior):

Incident #1   **Date:**   **Time:**

What occurred right before the behavior? (Include what you did.)

What occurred right after the behavior? (Include your own responses.)

Incident #2   **Date:**   **Time:**

What occurred right before the behavior? (Include what you did.)

What occurred right after the behavior? (Include your own responses.)

Incident #3   **Date:**   **Time:**

What occurred right before the behavior? (Include what you did.)

What occurred right after the behavior? (Include your own responses.)

Incident #4   **Date:**   **Time:**

What occurred right before the behavior? (Include what you did.)

What occurred right after the behavior? (Include your own responses.)

Incident #5   **Date:**   **Time:**

What occurred right before the behavior? (Include what you did.)

What occurred right after the behavior? (Include your own responses.)

Summarizing the incidents

Looking at your records of incidents above, what patterns do you see in the antecedents?

What is your ratio of rewards to punishments?

What patterns do you see in the consequences?

Were developmental expectations of your child appropriate in the situation?

   (Remember that even the seemingly no-demand situation of free time actually imposes demands in that the child must be able to initiate an appropriate activity.)

11

Look for Patterns

In the next few sections you will look for patterns in the behavior, noticing what comes before the behavior (antecedents) and what comes after the behavior (consequences). You will try to understand what function the behavior serves for your child, and this will help you to find more positive behaviors that your child can learn instead, that will serve the same purpose. For example, if your child likes to throw anything within reach, perhaps an appropriate behavior of throwing a foam ball or beanbag into a box can be taught instead. See the section on seeking sensory stimulation on page 74, for more ideas. It has a list of sensory equivalent substitutes for undesirable behaviors. All of this will be described in more detail in the sections that follow.

General patterns

Does the behavior occur more frequently at certain times of day (e.g., morning, afternoon, evening, before meals, after meals, before bed, after bed, after getting home from school, etc.).

Does the behavior occur more frequently during certain times of the week (e.g., beginning of the week, end of the week, weekends or weekdays)?

Does the behavior occur more frequently at certain times of the year (e.g., winter vs. summer, holiday times, returning to school after being on vacation, etc.)?

Are there certain places where the behavior occurs more frequently (e.g., in public vs. at home, certain rooms of the house, certain types of stores, parks, etc.)?

Who is more likely present when the behavior occurs (e.g., father vs. mother, males vs. females, familiar people vs. unfamiliar people, many people vs. few people, children vs. adults, people with loud voices vs. people with quiet voices, etc.)?

What kinds of environments are associated with the behavior (e.g., quiet vs. noisy, lots of activity vs. little activity, outdoors vs. indoors, kinds of lighting – bright, dim, fluorescent, etc.)?

What kinds of activities are taking place when the behavior occurs (e.g., when asked to do something, when engaged in certain activities, when child has free time, when interrupted, when told "no," "not yet," etc.)?

Are activities at the child's developmental level (or is too much being expected)?

12

Identify the Function of the Behavior

It is very important to identify the function the undesirable behavior serves. The function the behavior serves will tell you how to respond to it in order to make it more likely that it will decrease. The same behavior can serve different functions for different children. Even for the same child, the same behavior can serve different functions at different times.

As described in section 9, challenging behavior could serve some of the following functions:

- a way to escape or avoid an undesirable task or situation, e.g., one that is too difficult (beyond the child's developmental level)

- sensory stimulation (either overwhelmed with too much, or wanting more tactile (touch), kinesthetic (movement and position), visual (vision), auditory (hearing), gustatory (taste) or olfactory (smell) stimulation)

- relief from boredom (available activities are too easy or too hard; child does not know how to initiate activity without help from someone else)

- asking for attention

- expressing frustration with having no freedom to choose

- expressing frustration for other reasons

- expressing anger

- expressing fear of something (that may not be obvious to someone else)

- expressing that the child is not feeling good (illness, allergies, itching, medication side effects, fatigue, hunger, thirst, clothing too tight or tags irritating skin, earache, stomach ache, too much to eat, too warm or too cold, lighting is harsh or too dim, even though fine for adult)

- expressing impatience and not understanding that he or she has to wait

- expressing "No!"

- expressing "Wait! Let me finish!"

If the behavior is a means of escaping an undesirable situation, it would be important not to reward the child by allowing him or her to escape the situation as a result of the undesirable behavior, such as a tantrum.

If the situation is undesirable to the child because it is beyond his or her developmental level, then it is important to modify or eliminate the situation.

If the behavior is a bid for attention, it would be important not to reward it with attention, but instead to give attention when the child is behaving appropriately and to teach alternative means of asking for attention.

If the child is expressing or communicating something else, then the child needs to be taught alternative means of expressing or communicating that, whatever that is.

If the behavior is due to being overwhelmed with sensory stimulation, then the child needs to be given a place to retreat from sensory stimulation. If the behavior is due to the child not getting enough sensory stimulation, and the child is seeking sensory stimulation, then the child needs to be given alternative means of obtaining the sensory stimulation sought (see the list of sensory equivalent substitutes on pages 75–76).

If the child is behaving in an undesirable way because he or she is not feeling good, it would be important to monitor the child's physical state closely (e.g., take his or her temperature, check for ear infections, etc.) and to teach alternative means for the child to indicate that he or she is feeling bad.

And so on. Always look to find more positive behaviors that could serve the same function.

Function of the behavior

Consider the number one priority negative behavior that you selected earlier. What functions do you think the behavior serves?

If you wish, you can list the functions of the other negative behaviors you identified:

13

Use Rewards!

In setting up a behavior plan it is critical to identify the positive behaviors you want to replace the negative behaviors. If you reward the positive behaviors lavishly, and ignore the negative behaviors (unless they are a danger to the child or others or resulting in significant property destruction), the negative behaviors will start to drop away.

It is much more effective to focus on building positive behaviors than stamping out negative ones, although initially it may seem to take a little more effort. In reality, you probably spend more time reacting to negative behaviors than you would spend proactively responding to positive ones.

At first you may have to really look for the positive behaviors. They don't stand out as much as negative ones. Your child may not be engaging in them frequently, or may be engaging only in behavior that is somewhat remotely positive. You have to *catch him being good!*

Focusing on and responding to the good behavior and ignoring the negative really involves a transformation in the way you think about your child. It may be difficult at first, but it can transform your whole relationship with your child. For example, if you want your child to stop fighting with his brother, the positive behavior would be for him to interact nicely with his brother. You may notice this happens only for a few minutes at a time. Or you may notice that the closest thing to interacting nicely is that the two of them happen to be in the same room for a few minutes without fighting. That is what you have to reward. You may even have to teach them how to play a game, and reward them for doing so without fighting.

At first, you may find the negative behavior increasing when you ignore it and attend only to the positive behavior. It is as though the child is thinking, "This always got their attention before, I'll just do it again a little harder and longer." This is the time when you really have to persevere! They may not actually be thinking that, but their behavior will be the same as if they were. This is completely normal, and when you persist in ignoring the negative and attending only to the positive, this "extinction burst," as it's called in the behavior literature, subsides.

Remember that attention is usually rewarding, even if it is negative attention. When you ignore negative behavior, make sure you ignore it completely. For example, you may have to retreat behind a book (even if you aren't really reading it) to keep yourself from making eye contact, giving dirty looks, giving one-line reminders, warnings, etc.

See Appendix 1 for a list of rewards to use. For many children, attention and praise will be sufficient, but for many others you will need to back up your attention and praise with other kinds of rewards. The list in Appendix 1 gives a broad range of different kinds of rewards, so that you can rotate rewards. Sometimes rewards lose their effectiveness when used too often. To summarize:

- Look for the positive and reward it lavishly and enthusiastically.

- Ignore the negative, and when you ignore the negative, make sure you totally ignore it.

- Be ready for the extinction burst.

- Rotate rewards.

14

Create a Behavior Plan, Part 1: Antecedents, Communication, Structure, and Choice

In the following pages you will develop a behavior plan for *one* negative behavior you have identified. You will need to go through the same process for every other negative behavior you identify. You may want to make copies of the following pages so you will have them if you want to develop behavior plans for other behaviors.

Antecedents

Go back and look at the antecedents to the behavior that you identified. Some antecedents are further back in time than others. For example, if a child is upset over something that happened the day before, that event could be an antecedent to undesirable behavior. Some antecedents are more general than others. Some people speak of "setting events," which are more general and may be further removed in time than antecedents. Some common antecedents/setting events are:

Lack of rewards

If your child is getting more reprimands and time-outs than rewards for good behavior, then you will need to find a way to "catch him being good," and reward him or her more frequently. There should be at least five times as many rewards as reprimands/time-outs.

Lack of attention

If your child is not getting enough attention, you will have to find a way to spend more time with him or her. For many children, routine is important. You may establish a predictable time to spend with your child, and this may help him or her to understand, when he or she is alone, that there will be times later on when he or she will get some attention.

Sensory overload

If having too many people around is an antecedent, then you will need to avoid those situations, or provide your child with a retreat.

Sensory seeking

If seeking a certain kind of sensory stimulation seems to be involved, then you will need to find an appropriate sensory equivalent (see the section on seeking sensory stimulation on page 74). Note: some children experience both sensory overload *and* sensory seeking.

Disliked activities (for whatever reason)

If there are certain activities that tend to lead to the behavior, then you will have to find a way to make the activity more palatable (e.g., by rewarding each step), or drop the activity.

Developmental expectations

If the activity or expectation (e.g., too much unstructured time) is not at your child's developmental level, it needs to be modified or dropped.

Communication

Negative behavior is often due to the frustration of being unable to communicate. What communication system does your child use? How recently has he or she had a speech/language evaluation?

When evaluating a communication system, consider the following: memory and other cognitive demands; flexibility; practicality; the child's preferred modality; and encouragement of functional communications such as "Help," "Play with me," "Stop," "No," "Wait," "Hurts," and the like. Such functional commands are often more important than just labeling objects.

Structure

Structure is often very helpful to children in managing their behavior, particularly children with developmental disabilities. Structure includes predictability, routines, doing certain things in the same place and/or at the same time, having the environment physically uncluttered, and having visual cues as to what to do next.

For many children, even leisure must be structured. For example, it may be helpful to have a small box of toys with a routine for playing with each toy, and spend time with your child to teach him or her the routine. With enough coaching, your child may begin to get the box and play independently. Have a "finished" box in which your child can place each toy when done with it, to further structure the experience. This is a strategy used by the TEACCH program in North Carolina USA. See the earlier sections of this workbook on not knowing how to initiate appropriate activity, page 78.

Look over the page you completed on going through a typical day. Think about your schedule. How much routine is built into your day? In what ways could you make the day more structured for your child?

Transitions and change

Transitions and change are related to structure. Having things the same may be important for some children to understand the structure and to feel that things are predictable. A sense of predictability and stability may be important for them to feel safe. Many children with diagnoses on the autism spectrum have challenges with transitions and change. Children with mental retardation may also have challenges in this area. For ideas on how to handle this, see the sections on lack of flexibility and transitions on pages 131 and 133.

Using the TV or videos

Some children, particularly those with a diagnosis on the autism spectrum, may have certain videos or parts of videos that they like to watch over and over. The child may keep from getting into trouble while watching, but parents may feel guilty about allowing their child to spend too much time in this repetitive behavior.

As with the use of self-stimulation as a reward, discussed earlier, there may be another way to think about this. Unless you have another activity to offer your child and the time to supervise it, it may be unreasonable to deprive your child of something she enjoys and that gives her a feeling of security and predictability. Having at times made efforts to help your child play in more "meaningful" ways, it may be more realistic to allow her at other times to watch the video if that is what she wants.

It is also important to consider your own sanity and harmony within the family. If your child is being "good" while watching a video or TV, and that gives your family a reprieve from dealing with negative behavior, that is worth a good deal. As long as you know you are making efforts to teach your child alternative leisure activities some of the time (and school should be involved in this, too, so you don't have to do it all alone), don't be too hard on yourself if your child chooses the repetitive behaviors more than you would like. After all, most of us like to "space out" sometimes and, for example, watch a dumb TV show that does not particularly uplift us or teach us new things.

Behavior plan, part I: Antecedents/Setting events

The undesirable behavior of most concern that I am choosing for this behavior plan is (define objectively and measurably):

In finding a strategy to deal with the antecedent, remember the factors discussed above, and the function of the behavior. You may find that general setting events or situations are more relevant than specific antecedents, or you may find the reverse, or you may find that both are important. Fill out whichever applies:

Antecedent/setting event #1   Strategy to deal with it

Antecedent/setting event #2   Strategy to deal with it

Antecedent/setting event #3   Strategy to deal with it

Antecedent/setting event #4   Strategy to deal with it

Communication

Last speech/language evaluation was on _____

Use this communication system (e.g., pictures, signs, words, assistive communication device):

Work on these functional commands (e.g., help, play with me, fun, stop, it hurts, no, etc.):

Structure

What times of the day are most challenging?
1.

2.

What times of the week are most challenging?

3.

4.

How could you make it a little more structured at those times? Think about the following:

- routines

- doing certain things always in the same place

- doing certain things always at the same time

- having the environment physically uncluttered

- visual cues as to what to do next

- hand-over-hand support for how to get started

- verbal directions for how to get started (two-three word phrases)

- hand-over-hand support for what to do next

- verbal directions for what to do next (two-three word phrases).

Structure to try for time #1 (most challenging times, listed above)

Structure to try for time #2

Structure to try for time #3

Structure to try for time #4

Choices

Does my child like choices, or are choices overwhelming?

When does my child have choices about:

- what to do?

- what to wear?

- what to eat?

- who to be with?

- where to play?

- other?

Where are some places I could try building in choices for my child?

Choice

In a way, choice is the flip side of structure. Structure channels the child to help him or her learn and achieve self-control. But choice is important also. Giving a child a choice between two or more alternatives may be overwhelming in some situations, but in other situations, it may be just what is needed. More than two choices may be overwhelming for many children in many situations.

15

Create a Behavior Plan, Part 2: Reward Desirable Behaviors

What are the positive behaviors you would like to see instead of the negative behavior you have identified? As discussed earlier, some examples would be: if your child screams, you might like him to talk at a moderate volume, instead; if your child throws things, you might like her to put them down carefully, instead; if your child hits his siblings, you might like him to greet appropriately, share toys, etc., instead; if your child gets upset at having to make a transition, you might like her to make a smooth transition, instead.

Think about the number one priority negative behavior you have identified. Look at the function or functions that it serves, which you identified earlier. For each function of that negative behavior, identify a positive behavior or behaviors that you would like to see instead of the negative behavior.

Now look back at the section on rewards, and think of a way you could reward this replacement, positive behavior.

Give verbal feedback, *at your child's level*, as to why she is getting a reward, e.g., "nice playing," "you're trying hard," "nice smile," "good sharing," etc. Keep the comments short and give them immediately when the positive behavior happens. Don't give a dissertation on the value of pro-social behavior, just say "nice playing!" You are well on your way to building a behavior plan!

Behavior plan, part 2: Rewards

My child's negative behavior that this plan is addressing is (should be the same behavior that you worked with in the previous section):

The positive, replacement behavior(s) I would like to see my child engage in instead is (are):

The ways I will reward the positive behavior are:

16

Create a Behavior Plan, Part 3: Contingencies for Negative Behaviors

Ignore minor misbehaviors. Pick your battles! Highlight the negative behavior so it becomes salient to your child.

- Label it, if your child can understand a label.

- At a neutral time (when your child is not misbehaving) tell your child you want him to reduce this behavior, if he can understand language at that level.

- Give immediate feedback when the negative behavior occurs.

- Get the child's attention, and say "No!" using a stern tone of voice.

Immediately teach the positive, alternative behavior you have identified, if the child is not out of control.

Another strategy is to use a "cool-off" period, presented in a very calm and neutral fashion. Try to use the cool-off place *before* the child gets out of control and engages in negative behavior. The cool-off place should be distinct from time-out, so use a different place than you use for time-out. Use it when you see your child is getting wound up and needs some time and space to collect himself. You can stay with him and help soothe him at those times.

The strategy of "time-out" is probably the one most people know about, but it is the one that should be used the least. Use time-out as a last resort. Use it *only* for behaviors that are dangerous to self or others, severely disruptive, or could cause significant property damage; otherwise use rewards for the substitute positive behavior(s).

"Time-out" is short for "time out from positive reinforcement." It means placing the child in a safe place where he will not get attention or be able to engage in rewarding behaviors, for a brief period of time. Time-out does not teach the child what he should be doing instead of the negative behavior. Time-out often functions as punishment even though it is not supposed to be. "You catch more flies with honey than vinegar" really applies here.

When you feel you must use time-out, for danger to self, others, or severe property damage, proceed as follows:

- Say "No!" as described above, and then take your child to time-out.

- Do not make eye contact or otherwise give any attention when putting your child in time-out, otherwise it will not be time-out! (He will be getting attention.)

- Do not discuss the behavior before or during the time-out, otherwise it will not be time-out!

The rule of thumb is one minute of time-out per year of child's *mental* age.

The time-out area must be safe, and free of rewards that could cancel its effectiveness. For some children, being put in their room functions as time-out, even though their room is full of toys. For other children, being sent to a room full of toys functions as a treat. The important thing is how the setting functions for your child. Some children will sit in a chair facing the corner. Others will refuse to stay seated. If so, immediately place the child back in time-out each time he leaves. Do not speak to him or make eye contact while doing this. Restart the timer.

Use reverse time-out for a child who does not comply with being put in time-out, even when you keep returning him to time-out, as described above, or who is too big/strong to keep redirecting back to time-out.

- This means you leave the area.

- Monitor from an adjoining room if necessary.

- Do not give eye contact or other attention during the time-out.

- Do not discuss your child's behavior before or during the time-out.

Make sure rewards are used at least – 0 times more than reprimands and time-outs.
Considering the above strategies (ignoring, redirecting to positive behavior, using a cool-off place before behavior gets out of control, and as a last resort, using time-out), come up with a plan to follow when the negative behavior occurs. Your plan may have several steps (e.g., ignoring at first), or several contingencies, depending how severe the behavior is. Remember, time-out is only as a last resort for extremely serious behaviors (danger to self/others, property damage).

Behavior plan, part 3: What to do if the negative behavior occurs

17

Summarize Your Behavior Plan

Go over the sections on creating a behavior plan, Parts 1, 2, and 3. You can summarize your plan below.

Behavior plan summary

This plan addresses the following behavior (define in objective and measurable terms):

Having the following function(s):

Address antecedents/setting events:

Increase communication:

Create structure:

Give choices:

Reward the following replacement behaviors:

Rewards to be used:

Consequences for negative behaviors:

Review your plan:
Is it practical, i.e., can it be used consistently?

Is the behavior to be addressed clearly defined?

Does everyone involved agree with the plan?

PART VI

FINAL THOUGHTS

18

Strategies for Common Challenges

Getting into trouble

Children often get into trouble (making things messy, destroying things) when they can't organize themselves to do something more appropriate (see "Difficulty with organization needed to initiate an appropriate activity" on page 78).

Discover the function of the behavior and find acceptable substitutes

Your child may be getting various payoffs from the undesirable activities she gets into instead of initiating an appropriate play routine or other appropriate behavior. Some of those payoffs could include sensory stimulation (appealing sights, sounds, or tactile sensations), attention due to the disruption she causes, escape from requests, avoidance of requests that are beyond her capabilities, relief from boredom, etc.

If the payoff is sensory stimulation, your child may be getting enjoyable sensory stimulation from undesirable activities such as playing with people's hair. As discussed earlier on page 75, you can experiment to find out what substitutes you may be able to make, and then be consistent about never allowing the undesirable behavior. Instead, redirect her to the acceptable substitute. A soft brush may substitute for a person with a brush-cut hairdo. A pillow with silky fringe or a yarn doll may substitute for someone with longer hair. See page 75 for more ideas.

If the payoff is attention due to the disruption, make sure you are giving your child enough attention when she is behaving well. Some parents set a timer to ring every 15–20 minutes, to remind them to "catch her being good," and give praise, small edibles, stickers, etc. to reward good behavior.

If the payoff is escape from requests, make sure that your child has to complete the request and don't allow yourself to be distracted by disruptive behavior. Also make sure that your request is within your child's capabilities. Children often avoid demands that are beyond them. Think about the language level, cognitive level (e.g., memory and sequencing), and motor skills required. Try such strategies as breaking the task down into smaller parts, making the request one step at a time instead of a long string of language, providing some physical guidance, gently getting the child started, etc., and see what happens.

If the payoff is escape from boredom, setting up the independent play routines described above should help (see pages 78–79).

Reward her sibling for telling her to stop

Reward her sibling for saying simply, "stop." Praise her sibling and explain that she is being a big girl by helping her sister to learn good manners. It is important that her sibling be consistent in telling her "stop" and then redirecting her to an appropriate behavior. If her sibling does it only some of the time, it will just encourage her to continue.

Reward good behavior lavishly and often

As described above, reward appropriate behavior frequently. Think about what positive behaviors you want to see instead of the negative behaviors you don't want to see, and reward the positive behaviors. Generate a menu of rewards your child enjoys so that you can maintain the effectiveness of the rewards by rotating them, and by giving your child choices among the rewards (see Appendix 1).

Use time-out as a last resort

Use the above positive strategies and, as discussed earlier, use time-out only as a last resort for serious behaviors such as aggression. When you do use it, be consistent in always using it for that behavior. Always use it immediately, and do not give a warning first. A warning may confuse her because that means sometimes she is allowed to do the behavior and sometimes not. Use time-out for no more than a very few minutes at a time (a rule of thumb is one minute for every year of her *mental* age). If time-out is in the living room and it is not effective, consider using her bedroom (with the door ajar so you can see her without her knowing you are there). As discussed earlier, use a place for time-out that does not allow access to rewarding activities such as TV or computer games.

Self-esteem

Some children have trouble feeling good about themselves, for a variety of reasons. Many children with disabilities often experience failure and infrequently experience success. They may observe that peers are able to do things that they can't. They may have trouble expressing themselves verbally, participating in social situations, and performing academic tasks. Peers and adults may react to them in negative ways. Low self-esteem may be at the root of aggressive and other misbehavior, because the child is frustrated with failure.

Challenges with self-esteem can be addressed in two basic ways: building self awareness, acceptance and esteem within the child, and building a supportive community of children and adults around the child.

Building self awareness, acceptance, and esteem within the child
Ensure many experiences of success

Work with the child at his developmental level. He should experience at least five times as many successes as failures. If this is not the case, keep backing down to a lower level, breaking tasks into smaller parts, helping the child with the first step, and otherwise simplifying, until this rate of success occurs.

Think about your own life. Most people spend considerable time doing basically familiar tasks and consequently experience frequent successes in their jobs, with only the occasional failure, from which they can learn and develop new skills. Although many of us enjoy being challenged and pushing to the limits of what we can do, being continuously pushed beyond our capabilities and frequently failing would be frustrating. This can be so even when we are aware that we are pushing ourselves on purpose, in order to move ahead. Children must be given the opportunity to exercise the skills they have, so they can experience frequent success. They can't be expected to be always learning new skills.

Create and read a "Who am I" book

A "Who am I" book can be created with pictures from magazines, photographs, or drawings the child makes. Some suggestions for "chapters" are "things I'm good at," "things people like about me," "my family," "my pets," "my favorite things to do," "my favorite videos," and "my room." You may come up with other ideas for chapters, but those first two chapters are very important to include. Making those qualities explicit for a child who has experienced many failures and frustrations, and who has challenges socializing with peers, is very important. It may be valuable for the child to look at this book every day.

Create ways for the child to help others

Helping others is good for anyone's self-esteem. Try to find ways that the child can help at home, help his teachers, and help children at school, perhaps those who are younger.

Discuss the concept of individual differences

For those whose language is sufficiently advanced, discuss the idea that everyone has strengths and weaknesses, that there is nothing wrong or bad about having a weakness, that all anyone can do is make sure they do their best, whatever that is. There is always someone who will be better at anything we might do.

Build social skills

Having friends who care about them helps people to feel good about themselves. There are many programs and techniques available for building social skills. (See pages 42–43, 47–48, 129, and Appendix 2.)

Building a supportive community around the child

Circles of Friends, by Robert and Martha Perske, describes how friendship groups can be created in schools and other settings, consisting of an individual with disabilities and more typically developing peers. These groups have benefits for all members.

"Understanding Friends" is an eight-page program by Catherine Faherty of the Asheville, North Carolina TEACCH program, available on the Internet at http://www.teacch.com/undrstfr.htm. (Note that "teacch" has two "c"s.) This program includes experiential exercises to help typically developing children develop empathy for and understanding of children with disabilities.

Talk to your child's class. Some parents visit their child's class and talk to the children, explaining their child's disability and behavior, and helping children understand the best ways to interact with the child and how they can help.

You may have to do some education of the staff at your child's class before you get to the point of educating your child's classmates. *Circles of Friends* might be a good book to give your child's school staff (principal, director of special education, etc.) if they are not already familiar with it. Keep in mind that federal law requires a free and appropriate public education for every child, and that the least restrictive educational setting is also required by law. It is your child's legal right to be included as much as possible, and to be treated with respect and kindness. Bullying and being treated unkindly is certainly not part of an appropriate education.

Helping your child stay calm

The following are suggestions for types of stimulation that may help your child to calm him or herself. Some stimuli may not have the desired effect for some children. You may have to experiment to find the right stimuli for your child.

Absence of irritating stimuli

- tags on shirts and other articles of clothing
- elastic waistbands and wrists
- clothing that is too tight
- wool (feels scratchy and irritating to some children)
- dressed too warmly or not warmly enough
- noise, high-pitched sounds
- bright/harsh lights, fluorescent lights, flickering lights (some children may notice a flicker that most of us do not notice)
- fabric of upholstery or clothing that is irritating to the child.

Motion

- rocking chair
- rocking horse
- swing
- "sit and spin"
- riding in a wagon
- trike/bike
- jumping (trampolines need spotters standing around all the edges at all times to catch the child if he or she falls or trips).

Music

- soothing, new age (but some may find it irritating)
- lively music (but some may become more active)
- some may like headphones (but some may be irritated by them)
- children's songs
- lullabies
- try different styles of music – borrow from the library to try out lots of styles.

Sounds

- white noise generator
- sound of fan running
- tape of sounds child enjoys
- bells
- someone talking.

Visual motion

- motion lamp (like "lava lamps")
- video of logs burning in a fireplace
- videotapes.

Tactile

- fuzzy, velvety stuffed toys, blankets, or articles of clothing
- water play
- play with dried beans
- sandbox
- hand cream/lotion
- play dough
- "fiddle object" – small toy to hold in hand
- back rubs/massage – deep pressure usually works best; light pressure can be irritating.

Vibration

- leaning against dryer or washer
- riding in car.

Enclosure/confinement/pressure

- pop-up tent
- large appliance carton (e.g., refrigerator, washer) – fix up with pillows

- card table with blanket over it (child can crawl under)

- space behind the couch

- wrapping up in a large towel or blanket

- weighted vest

- beanbag chair

- hugs and cuddling (but some children find this irritating).

Personal space

- having sufficient personal space for child and belongings.

Scents

- cologne

- herbs

- scented sachets

- scented candles (but candles and matches can be hazardous for some).

Oral

- plastic tubing to chew on

- chewing gum (if child would not swallow it)

- chewy foods, e.g., jerky, fruit leather, crunchy foods.

Playing with peers: Peer interaction games

All children want to be connected with people, and enjoy having fun with other people; however, sometimes children with developmental disabilities need some extra coaching and guidance in learning about the fun of interacting with other people. Sometimes the child's language level, limited understanding of social rules, and behaviors can make this more challenging to learn than it is for most children. Below are some ideas for fostering interaction between your child and another child, whom you will teach to help your child.

Initially, you will probably have to supervise the interaction, but as your helper child becomes more skilled, she will need less and less help and guidance from you.

Note: For simplicity, the child with a developmental disability will be referred to as "your child," or "he," and the other child will be referred to as the "helper child," or "she."

Tug-of-war

Use a scarf, sash, towel, or other long piece of fabric. Place one end in your child's hands, and tell the helper child to hold the other end. You may have to help your child hang on to the scarf. Then tell the helper child to gently tug and to respond with smiles and excited comments when your child looks at her. Tell her to stop tugging and wait for your child to indicate that he wants her to start tugging again, by looking at her, gesturing, vocalizing, or reciprocating the tug. This game should be supervised so that no one gets tangled up in or choked by the sash. Put it away in a safe place when the supervised play session is finished.

Rolling a ball back and forth

Variations: throwing a ball or beanbag back and forth.

Tell the helper child to get the child's attention before rolling or throwing. When the child retrieves the ball or beanbag, tell her to clap and get excited; she may then have to go over to him and position his arms to make the throw or roll to her. She may have to stay very close to accomplish this.

Riding in a wagon

Variations: pushing in a box or wheeled chair (e.g., office desk chair).

Have your child get in the wagon, box, or chair. Tell the helper child to pull the wagon gently (or push the box or chair). When your child laughs or notices the movement, tell the helper child to respond by smiling, laughing, making excited comments, etc. Then tell her to stop, and wait for the child to indicate he wants more, by looking at her, gesturing, vocalizing, bouncing, etc.

After a few turns, have the children change places. At first the child may resist this. If so, have the helper child cut short her turn in the wagon/box/chair, before returning the child to the wagon/box/chair. You may have to use hand-over-hand assistance to encourage the child to pull the wagon (or push the box or chair). When the child does pull or push, tell the helper child to exaggerate her responses, e.g., lots of smiling, laughing, and excited comments. Tell her to try to make eye contact with the child while she responds. As the child learns that he is the cause of the helper child's enjoyment, he may gradually be willing to stay longer in the puller/pusher role.

Blowing bubbles

Have the helper child blow bubbles. Tell her to make sure the child is watching before starting. Tell her to catch a bubble on the wand and move it in front of the child. Before blowing again, tell her to try to wait for the child to indicate he wants more, by making eye contact with her, by gestures, or by vocalizing.

Building a tower of blocks

Have the helper child begin building a tower of blocks. Then indicate to your child to place another block on the tower. When he does so, the helper child can say "your turn." The helper child can respond positively to that, and then say, "my turn," while placing another block of her own. Then she can repeat the process.

If your child is able to look at block diagrams and copy the structures, they could do something more advanced than just a tower. But they should follow the same format of "my turn," "your turn," etc.

Lack of flexibility: Insistence on sameness, and having to have things a certain way

Some children, and many children with a diagnosis of autism or Pervasive Developmental Disorder–Not Otherwise Specified (PDD–NOS), may display very narrow interests, seem to be obsessed with certain items, and be very resistant to change or to things not being or happening just as they believe they should. For a child with language and/or perceptual challenges, the world may be confusing and unpredictable. This need for control and having things a certain way may be the child's way of trying to make a confusing world more predictable and understandable.

The general strategy in dealing with this is "accommodate and stretch," i.e., recognize that the child has a need for order and predictability, and try to accommodate this need. However, when this need creates undue family stress, or gets in the way of the child's development and well-being, then some limits must be set and the child must be gently encouraged to "stretch" a bit: to expand the behavioral repertoire, and to learn to tolerate some variations.

There may be some tantrums, but future battles may be less intense after the child has gone through it once. It will also help the child to realize that some changes can occur without the world falling apart. As long as the changes are done thoughtfully and gently, not too many at once, and the child is still accommodated in other areas, parents and teachers should remain firm and know that the tantrums will eventually cease and everyone will be fine.

Some parents purposely vary routines just a little bit each day so that a child does not get too entrenched in certain routines. You will have to balance this with the child's need for structure and predictability. You will have to discover when to do things always exactly the same, and when to introduce variation. Every family has to find this balance for themselves. See Lorna Wing, *The Autistic Spectrum* (2001), for a discussion of this point.

Pick some situation or behavior where you would like to see more flexibility. Find a way to introduce something that is novel, but not too novel, and then reward compliance. The reward could be a preferred food, a sticker, blowing some bubbles, a noisemaker the child enjoys, a pat on the back, or some other easily dispensable reward that does not take the child away from the task at hand for more than a moment or two. Some examples are given below.

Lining up toys but not playing with them

You could join the child in the activity and help her line them up. Then, introduce a novel action with the toys. For example, if the child only lines up toy cars and does not play with them, you could roll one of the cars so that it knocks something over. You could say "boom!" to make the action more interesting. Repeat this action, and observe whether the child is interested. If not, keep repeating the action over a period of days. When the child begins to show some interest, encourage her, with hand-over-hand assistance, if necessary, to perform this action. Reward compliance immediately. Don't expect the child to incorporate these new actions immediately, but if you keep repeating this activity several times a week, the child may eventually do so on her own. Then you can start to introduce other actions.

Eating foods of only a certain color

You could use food coloring to make a novel food one of the child's preferred colors. Reward the child for eating a bite of it. Then give another reward for eating two or more bites. Gradually use less and less food coloring.

Not sharing toys

Start with a toy that the child is not so insistent on keeping all to herself. You may encourage sharing by taking the toy for only a moment, and then returning it to her but rewarding lavishly for "sharing." Then move to a slightly more preferred toy and reward for sharing that.

Watching only certain videotapes

Introduce another videotape that is in a similar vein. Find a section of the tape which you think will have something of interest. Point it out by labeling excitedly. Expect the child to watch the new video for at least 30–60 seconds before being allowed to watch the preferred one. Use rewards to motivate compliance. Give lots of praise when the child watches the new video. Don't expect her to watch more than a few minutes, at first. Gradually, as it becomes more familiar, she may be willing to watch it for longer periods. Do this regularly, at least two or three times a week, so that the video has a chance to become familiar. You could also make "new videos" part of a routine, e.g., watching a new video for a minute before the preferred one each time. For some children, labeling it as "new video" time may be helpful.

Playing alone

The child likes to do form puzzles, as many children with autism do. Turn this into an opportunity to expand the child's repertoire a bit, and practice turn-taking. Turn-taking is an important skill in language development and social development. Put the puzzle pieces in a stack and give the child one to place, saying, "your turn." Then you take the next piece and put it in place, saying, "my turn." Then give her another piece, saying, "your turn," and so on.

As you can see from these examples, the idea is to gently stretch what the child is doing, just a little bit, and to reward it liberally and immediately. As the child gets gently introduced to new activities and ideas, she will probably eventually start incorporating some of them spontaneously into her life, and future changes may be more easily accepted.

Picture schedules

Picture schedules may be a good way to incorporate changes. For example, watching a new video before seeing a familiar one, as described above, could be incorporated into a picture schedule of the after-school routine. Picture schedules can be made from magazine pictures, drawings, or actual photographs of the child in the activity, or photos or colored copies of the pictures on the video box (best for children whose abstract thinking skills are not sufficient to generalize from a magazine picture or a drawing).

Transitions

Most of us find change and transition to be somewhat challenging. For many individuals with intellectual disabilities and/or autism, transitions can be unusually challenging. Listed below are some suggestions that may help to ease these transitions. Some of the suggestions may be more applicable than others to particular individuals.

1. *Respect the difficulty of making the transition* and try to empathize. Imagine something like moving overseas to begin life in a new country. That's

how disoriented a person with intellectual disabilities or autism may *feel* when faced with a "simple" transition.

2. *Analyze transitions* in terms of people, places, activities, and objects. Are there some kinds of transitions that are particularly troublesome to the child? For example, do changes in location bother the child very little, but changes in people really upset him or her? Once you have this information, see whether there is some way to make those particular kinds of transitions less frequent, or to make those changes only when as many other aspects of the situation as possible can be held constant.

3. *Transition objects/transition people.* This is related to the preceding point. Sometimes it helps if a person can carry a favorite object or toy from one place to the next, or keep it throughout different situations. It may also help if a familiar person can accompany the person into the new situation, at least until they have a little time to adjust.

4. *Previewing.* Let the child know what is coming up. Talk about it beforehand, for example, the day before. During the day, remind the child what will happen and when. (This assumes the individual is cognitively capable of comprehending this. If not, pictures may work. See #5.) You will have to determine how far in advance to start talking about the change. Some children may become overwhelmed with anxiety if you start talking about it a week or even a day in advance. For some transitions, previewing it 5–10 minutes ahead of time may work best (see #7 below). It depends on the individual, and the particular transition.

5. *Use a schedule.* One way to preview is to have a schedule, either a written one or a pictorial one. This is where a child's love of routine can pay off. If he knows the schedule, he knows when the transitions are coming, and it can become part of his routine. For changes from the usual schedule, use previewing. With someone whose language comprehension is limited, use pictures to help explain the unusual happening.

6. *Avoid upsetting antecedents.* As much as possible, try to allow time for the preceding activity to end before beginning the transition. Try to bring the activity to a natural closure before the transition takes place. Try to

avoid other conditions that may be upsetting to the individual even without a transition, e.g., loud noises.

7. *Give warnings.* Let the child know that a transition will be happening soon. For example, ten minutes before the change, set a timer for five minutes. When it goes off, remind him or her that the change will occur when the timer goes off again. Then set the timer for five minutes again.

8. *Use lavish praise* during the period immediately before a transition. Find things you can honestly praise, especially compliance with routines around concluding one activity prior to making the transition. This will create a positive mind-set for the child, reminding him or her how nice praise is, and making him or her not want to ruin it by getting upset with the transition!

9. *Make transitions slowly.* When it is time for the change, try to allow time so the process can be gentle and somewhat slow, rather than rushed and abrupt. Speak slowly and softly to the child, to let him or her know it is time for the change.

10. *Use simple, concrete language* at transition times. For many children with developmental disabilities, understanding language may be effortful and stressful. Therefore, it is particularly important not to use language that adds to the stress. For example, don't say, "It's your responsibility to put everything away in its proper place before we go to the gym." Do say, "Crayons in the box," "papers in the desk." Supplement with gestures if necessary.

11. *Give choices where possible.* If possible, allow a choice in activity following the transition, so the child maintains a feeling of some control in the situation. If possible, allow other choices, such as someone to accompany the child, or an object to take, or choice of a reward available for successfully completing the transition.

12. *Modeling.* Select someone who makes transitions smoothly and allow that person to be nearby so that he or she can be observed making a smooth transition.

13. *Relaxation/deep breathing.* Before the transition, ask the child to take a few deep breaths and say "relax." Take a few deep breaths yourself and

encourage imitation. Sometimes people who are severely and profoundly retarded can imitate taking a deep breath and benefit from this technique, even if they can't understand the language used. For children who *can* understand the language being used, it may be even easier to learn to do this.

14. *Reward smooth transitions.* Develop a "menu" of rewards that are motivating to the child. After a smooth transition, give one of those rewards. For those who can delay rewards, making transitions might be an item on a star chart. A certain number of stars can be "cashed in" later on for a reward. See Appendix 1.

15. *Positive self-talk* (for those who have the cognitive capabilities). Suggest that the child say to himself or herself what will happen next, and then say things like, "I'll be fine. I can do it. I can handle it."

Shopping strategies

- Make short shopping trips (10–15 minutes) and build up to longer trips as they are tolerated.

- Make a list of rules (rules must be short, two to three words at most), e.g.:
  - good hands (e.g., no grabbing, hitting)
  - good walking (e.g., don't run off, stay close to mom)
  - use your words.

- Prepare: go over the list of rules.

- Go over visual aids (map of shops if he would understand; pictures of the schedule).

- If the child is small enough, place him in the shopping cart or trolley.

- Use frequent (*at least* every five minutes) rewards for good behavior (e.g., sweets, raisins, if praise alone is not enough).

- Have the child hold your hand; put his other hand in his pocket.

- Interact as you go – follow his lead sometimes, comment on what he's interested in.

- Go at quieter, less crowded times.

- Use headphones and/or sunglasses to cut down stimulation; sing songs together if the child likes to sing.

- Take short breaks – sit somewhere to have a snack/play with toys.

- Give choices, if purchasing something.

- Use a routine: first we go here (where I want), then we go there (where you want).

- Explore other options, such as a park, if you use shopping just as an outing.

- If your child has a sibling, avoid having both children at once at the shops.

Haircuts, restaurants, visiting the doctor or dentist

Haircuts

Like many of the other strategies, the strategy here is to introduce components of the event in small doses before the day of the actual event. Snip scissors in the air near your child, gradually getting closer over a period of days or weeks. Take your child to the barber's or hair salon several times in advance, to get her used to the environment. If possible, introduce your child to the person who will be cutting her hair. Model snipping small pieces of hair from a sibling, if possible, or with the child's doll. Pair these hair snipping exercises with the child's favorite music, video, or snack. Bring these supports with you on the day of the hair-cutting.

Make sure scissors are out of reach or locked up except when you are using them in this way.

Restaurants

You can use some of the same strategies for restaurants. Often it works better to go at times when the restaurant is uncrowded. Sitting in a more secluded corner is sometimes helpful. Being near the doors to the kitchen, where there are more smells, movement, and noise, is probably the least desirable location. Going to smaller restaurants may help. Going to a restaurant for just a beverage or dessert may work better at first, then after the child is comfortable with doing this, go for an entire meal.

Taking entertainment for your child can be helpful, e.g., crayons and coloring books, puzzles, and a portable stereo.

Visiting the doctor

You can use the same kinds of techniques for visits to the doctor. Practice components ahead of time, take your child to the doctor's office to familiarize her with the environment, introduce her to the receptionist, nurse, and doctor, if possible, in advance. Pair the experience with positive ones.

Visiting the dentist

You can use many of the same techniques, but for some children, using sedatives or anesthetics is the only way that dental work can be performed. In small, rural communities, there may not be dentists available who are prepared to do this. Usually in larger towns and cities, you can find someone with this experience. You may want to contact a specialist organization if you need help finding someone (see Appendix 2).

Visiting relatives and friends

Take something familiar that your child likes, such as a favorite toy. Find a quieter corner for your child to play in, if noise and commotion tend to disturb your child. Supervise your child's play with other children, rather than expecting him to do it all alone. Take something to use as a retreat area, e.g., a large appliance container (folded flat for transporting), or a blanket that can be put over a table. A walkman may help your child to screen out noise. Another idea is to bring favorite videos and find a place for your child to watch them. Brief periods of socializing, and allowing the child to retreat the rest of the time, may work better than insisting he be present and interacting for the entire visit.

Having your child meet some of the people on his or her own turf, beforehand, may help.

Explaining to your relatives or friends what your child's issues and needs are, beforehand, may also help.

You may have to leave earlier than you would like. If you have two caregivers available, you may take two cars so that one can leave early, without the rest of the family having to leave. If you live close enough, you may be able to come back after a break.

There may be times when investing in a baby-sitter may be the best choice. You will have to weigh how important it is for your child to be present at this particular occasion, vs. what it will cost him and you.

Birthday parties

Many of the suggestions above may be applicable here. You may want to consider in particular going for a shorter period of time. It may be valuable for your child to have a short and sweet time at the party, rather than to stay for all of it and have it become a painful experience for him, and possibly for other children as well. Having a painful time may also make it harder to get him to go to the next one. Keep in mind that such parties may be noisy and unpredictable, which is very challenging for many children with a diagnosis on the autism spectrum. Pay special attention to finding ways to help your child retreat from the noise and commotion, and to make it structured and predictable as much as possible. Make sure the host or hostess understands something of your child's issues and needs, and stay through the party with your child, if possible. Taking a familiar toy or other object may help.

Conclusion

To conclude, I would like to reiterate some of the most important points I have tried to stress throughout this workbook.

See yourself as capable of having more positive interactions with your child. Remember that you are faced with a more demanding task than most parents, so if you are having challenges it does not reflect poorly on you at all. Just as you notice your child's successes and celebrate them, so you must celebrate your own. Notice the times you did something well, focus on them, and your skills will improve.

Find the people and behaviors that support you. Create a support network of people and find time for the things that recharge you. Give yourself what you need so you can keep on giving. Remember that your child has much to teach others, and so do you. You are not just needing support, but offering something of value in the process.

Be sure to rule out medical factors. Children with developmental disabilities may be limited in the ways they can communicate discomfort and distress. Their behavior may be caused by a medical condition that needs treatment.

Having ruled out medical issues, if your child is misbehaving, assume he or she is having difficulty with the expectations and try to simplify them. Learn to think analytically in terms of the many different skills involved in what might seem at first to be the most simple, uncomplicated task.

Understand your child's developmental levels in all areas. Don't think in terms of just one level. It's important to understand your child's abilities in all areas so you can better understand the functions served by undesirable behaviors and better know how to encourage the development of more positive behaviors. Although the undesirable behaviors tend to get attention, it is by focusing on the positive behaviors and rewarding them that you will have better outcomes in the long run, and more fun in the process.

Fun is important! Have fun with other people as well as with your child. When you're having fun, you have more energy, more creativity, and more tolerance for those inevitable times when things don't go well. You may find that your child leads you to have fun in ways you never would have thought of by yourself!

Appendix 1

Reward/Reinforcer Survey

As I have tried to illustrate throughout this book, identifying the behaviors you want to see, and rewarding them frequently, will cause them to increase and supplant the behaviors you don't want to see. This is more effective in the long run than responding only to behaviors you don't want to see. With that in mind, here are some ideas to get you thinking about rewards. Rewards do not have to be just food or objects. There are many possibilities. Some are listed below.

Note: Items included are for children and adults of all ages. Some of the items may not be appropriate for your child. Some of the items will lend themselves better than others to being used as rewards in teaching or behavior management situations with your child. Younger children may need frequent, small rewards that do not consume much time. Older children and adults may sometimes be able to go for longer periods without a reward, hence a more time-consuming activity, such as an excursion, could be a reward. Tokens can be used as an immediate consequence for good behavior, and they can be cashed in later for a reward, but only for children and adults who have the cognitive ability to understand a symbol, and who can defer gratification.

Social

For children with an autism spectrum disorder, social rewards alone may not be enough. If this is the case, don't hesitate to use other kinds of rewards. This is not a bad thing to do, as discussed earlier in the section on rewards. Whatever else you use, pair it with a social reward so that social rewards might eventually become more attractive to your child.

- being smiled at
- attention
- peer attention/approval (ask peers to notice child's good behavior)
- playing with others
- being praised
- being hugged
- clapping
- pat on the back

- pat on the hand
- pat on the head
- back rub
- being told "good work!" or "you're playing nicely!" or some other brief, positive comment
- high-fives, if the child understands/enjoys it
- thumbs up gesture, if the child understands it.

Food/beverages

Small items that can be easily and frequently dispensed, such as:

- raisins
- nuts
- cereal pieces, e.g., fruit loops
- pieces of cookies
- pieces of crackers
- sweets or candy
- sip of juice, soft drink, or chocolate milk.

Cut off a piece of refrigerated cookie dough and bake it on the spot, as a reward (if the child can understand what the reward is for after waiting for the cookie to bake).

Toys/games

- stickers and stars
- blocks
- Legos
- puzzles
- slinky toy
- toy cars and vehicles
- toy animals
- dolls
- puppets
- picture books
- electric trains
- bicycle
- board games
- card games
- checkers
- chess.

Visual

- mirrors
- shiny objects
- glittery objects
- moving objects
- mobile
- looking out the window at traffic
- looking at an aquarium
- looking at a motion/lava lamp
- looking at an overhead fan
- looking at a videotape of a fire in a fireplace, aquarium, etc.

Tactile/kinesthetic

- feeling something fuzzy, smooth, nubby or ribbed, e.g., fuzzy stuffed animals, wide-wale corduroy

- squeezing something soft

- feeling something squishy

- sitting or lying on soft pillows

- sitting or lying in a beanbag chair

- play dough

- hand lotion

- water play

- sand play

- bean bags

- being wrapped up tightly in a large towel or blanket

- feeling vibrations, such as a vibrating toy, the washing machine when running, or a vibrator

- having back rubbed

- having hair rumpled

- feeling a breeze from a miniature fan

- touching something very cold (e.g., "blue ice")

- touching something warm, e.g., heating pad or running drier (which has vibration in addition to warmth)

- being picked up and swung around

- piggy-back ride

- being pulled in a wagon

- being pulled in a large box

- opportunity to crawl into a secluded space, such as a large appliance box or pop-up tent (not really tactile or kinesthetic, but seems to fit here).

Olfactory

- colognes and perfumes

- scented hand lotion

- small containers of spices.

Entertainment

- watching television (favorite programs)
- watching videos (favorite videos)
- listening to music
- looking at catalogs
- reading
- playing with others.

Sports and physical activity

- tricycle
- scooter
- wagon
- rolling a ball back and forth with someone
- playing catch
- kicking a ball
- bouncing a ball
- trampoline (must have spotters to stand around the entire perimeter)
- jumping, skipping, and hopping
- playing "catch me"
- hide and seek
- beanbag toss (into a container)
- throwing a ball into a basket
- swinging
- sliding down a slide
- climbing on jungle gym
- bicycle
- swimming
- skating
- skiing
- playing football
- playing softball
- shooting baskets
- playing basketball
- horseback riding
- tennis
- hiking/walking
- running
- racing
- ping pong
- pool
- fishing.

Music, arts and crafts

- humming
- singing along to music
- singing alone or with others
- playing a musical instrument
- using rhythm instruments
- listening to favorite tapes/CDs
- chimes
- ringing a bell

- giving bell to individual to ring
- dancing
- working with clay or play dough
- finger painting
- drawing (crayons, markers, pencils, etc.)
- building models
- stringing beads.

Excursions

- riding in a car
- visiting grandparents or other relatives
- visiting friends
- visiting a beach

- visiting a zoo
- visiting a playground
- visiting a museum
- going out to eat
- going shopping.

Helping around the house

- setting the table
- making the bed
- washing the dishes
- putting clothes in the washing machine or dryer
- vacuuming
- sweeping
- wiping counters, tables, windows, etc.

- baking
- cooking
- working in the yard
- raking leaves
- repairing things
- taking something to someone
- delivering messages
- other errands.

Personal appearance

- getting new clothes
- dressing up in costumes
- dressing up in parent's clothes
- getting a haircut
- going to the beauty parlor.

Other events and activities

- being given a choice of activity or toy
- opportunity to open something or take apart something, e.g., put something appealing to the child in a box/container
- getting an allowance
- engaging in relaxation time (quiet place with soothing music)
- having a pet
- having a party
- going to a party
- staying up past bedtime
- having free time
- taking a bath/shower.

Appendix 2

Resources for Autism and Intellectual Disabilities

US organizations

The Arc (has local chapters)
Membership Department
1010 Wayne Avenue, Suite 650
Silver Spring
Maryland 20910
www.TheArc.org

The national organization of and for people with intellectual disabilities and related developmental disabilities and their families.

Autism Society of America (has local chapters)
7910 Woodmont Avenue, Suite 300
Bethesda
Maryland 20814-3067
www.autism-society.org

Serving the needs of individuals with autism and their families through advocacy, education, public awareness, and research since 1965.

The Behavior Home Page

A collaboration of the Kentucky Department of Education (KDE) and the Department of Special Education and Rehabilitation Counseling (SERC).

www.state.ky.us/agencies/behave/homepage.html

Products and ideas for sensory concerns

www.sensorycomfort.com
www.SensoryResources.com

This website contains resources for raising children with sensory motor, developmental, and social-emotional challenges. They specialize in sensory issues.

UK organizations

The Challenging Behaviour Foundation

32 Twydall Lane

Gillingham

Kent ME8 6HX

www.thecbf.org.uk

The CBF provides and accesses support, advice and information in addition to raising awareness of challenging behavior.

Foundation for People with Learning Disabilites

www.learningdisabilites.org.uk

Mission is to promote the rights, quality of life, and opportunities of people with learning disabilities and their families through research, spreading knowledge and information, supporting communities and services to include those with learning disabilites, and making practical improvements in services. Note that in the UK, "learning disability" means the same thing as "mental retardation" in the US.

National Autistic Society (NAS)

www.nas.org.uk

The NAS champion the rights and interests of all people with autism and ensure that they and their families receive quality services appropriate to their needs. The website includes information about autism spectrum disorders, the NAS and its services and activities.

Resources for Autism

858 Finchley Road

London NW11 6AB

www.resourcesforautism.org.uk

This organization provides a national advice and expert witness service.

Websites

American Association on Mental Retardation

www.aamr.org

This website contains information about the mental retardation and disabilities field; their goal is to build societal and professional capacity and the website has lists of resources. Note that in the UK, the term "learning disability" means the same thing as "mental retardation" in the US.

Family Village

www.familyvillage.wisc.edu/index.htmlx

A global community of disability-related resources.

The Gray Center for Social Learning and Understanding

Carol Gray provides lots of information on social skills, social stories, bullying, dealing with the playground and recess, etc. for children with diagnoses on the autism spectrum; also a newsletter and many publications.
www.thegraycenter.org

O.A.S.I.S. (Online Asperger Syndrome Information and Support)

www.udel.edu/bkirby/asperger

Treatment and Education of Autistic and Related Communication Handicapped Children (TEACCH)

www.teacch.com
Also "Understanding Friends" (see page 126 www.teacch.com/undrstfr.htm)

Lots of great, practical information.

Basic books for you and for educating others about autism

Attwood, Tony (1998) *Asperger's Syndrome: A Guide for Parents and Professionals.* London: Jessica Kingsley Publishers.

Grandin, Temple (1995) *Thinking in Pictures and Other Reports from My Life with Autism.* New York: Random House, Inc.

Grandin, Temple and Johnson, Catherine (2005) *Animals in Translation: Using the Mystery of Autism to Decode Animal Behavior.* New York: Scribner.

Gray, Carol (2000) *The New Social Story Book – Illustrated Edition.* Arlington, TX: Future Horizons, Inc.

Koegel, Robert L. and Koegel, Lynn Kern (1995) *Teaching Children with Autism: Strategies for Initiating Positive Interactions and Improving Learning Opportunities.* Bethesda, MD: Paul H. Brookes Publishing Co.

Parks, Clara (1967) *The Siege: The First Eight Years of an Autistic Child.* Boston: Little, Brown, and Co.

Parks, Clara (2001) *Exiting Nirvana: A Daughter's Life with Autism.* Boston: Little, Brown, and Co.

Siegel, Bryna (1996) *The World of the Autistic Child: Understanding and Testing Autistic Spectrum Disorders.* New York: Oxford University Press.

Siegel, Bryna (2003) *Helping Children with Autism Learn: Treatment Approaches for Parents and Professionals.* New York: Oxford University Press.

Wing, Lorna (2003) *The Autism Spectrum.* London: Constable and Robinson.

Basic books for you and for educating others about intellectual disabilities

Pueschel, Siegfried M. (1988) *The Special Child: A Source Book for Parents of Children with Developmental Disabilities.* Baltimore, MD: Paul H. Brookes Publishing Co.

Smith, Romayne (ed) (1993) *Children with Mental Retardation: A Parents' Guide.* Bethesda, MD: Woodbine House.

Social skills books

Gutstein, Steven, and Sheely, Rachelle (2002) *Relationship Development Intervention with Children, Adolescents and Adults: Social and Emotional Development Activities for Asperger Syndrome, Autism, PDD and NLD.* London: Jessica Kingsley Publishers.

Gutstein, Steven, and Sheely, Rachelle (2003) *Relationship Development Intervention with Young Children: Social and Emotional Development Activities for Asperger Syndrome, Autism, PDD and NLD.* London: Jessica Kingsley Publishers.

Heinrichs, Rebekah (2003) *Perfect Targets: Asperger's Syndrome and Bullying.* Shawnee Mission, KS: Autism Asperger Publishing Co.

McAfee, Jeanette L. (2001) *Navigating the Social World: A Curriculum for Individuals with Asperger's Syndrome, High Functioning Autism and Related Disorders.* Arlington, TX: Future Horizons, Inc.

MacDonald, James, D. (2004) *Communicating Partners: 30 Years of Building Responsive Relationships with Late Talking Children including Autism, Asperger's Syndrome (ASD), Down Syndrome and Typical Development. Developmental Guides for Professionals and Parents.* London: Jessica Kingsley Publishers.

Perske, Robert and Perske, Martha (1988) *Circles of Friends: People with Disabilities and Their Friends Enrich the Lives of One Another.* Nashville, TN: Abingdon Press.

Quill, Kathleen (2000) *Do-Watch-Listen-Say: Social and Communication Intervention for Children with Autism.* Baltimore, MD: Paul H. Brookes Publishing Co.

Sonders, Susan Aud (2002) *Giggle Time – Establishing the Social Connection: A Program to Develop the Communication Skills of Children with Autism.* London: Jessica Kingsley Publishers.

Skillstreaming series

Goldstein, Arnold P. and McGinnis, Ellen (1997) *Skillstreaming the Adolescent: New Strategies and Perspectives for Teaching Prosocial Skills.* Champaign, IL: Research Press.

McGinnis, Ellen and Goldstein, Arnold P. (1997) *Skillstreaming the Elementary School Child: New Strategies and Perspectives for Teaching Prosocial Skills.* Champaign, IL: Research Press.

McGinnis, Ellen and Goldstein, Arnold P. (2003) *Skillstreaming in Early Childhood: New Strategies and Perspectives for Teaching Prosocial Skills.* Champaign, IL: Research Press.

There are a wealth of books on social skills by Carol Gray and others at www.the-graycenter.org (see above under "Websites").

Books on behavior

Bambara, Linda M. and Knoster, T. (1998) *Designing Positive Behavior Support Plans.* Washington, DC: "Innovations" Research to Practice Series, #13. American Association on Mental Retardation.

Demchak, Mary Ann and Bossert, Karen W. (1996) *Assessing Problem Behaviors.* Washington, DC: "Innovations" Research to Practice Series, #4. American Association on Mental Retardation.

Durand, V. Mark (1998) *Sleep Better! A Guide to Improving Sleep for Children with Special Needs.* Baltimore, MD: Paul H. Brookes Publishing Co.

Fouse, Beth and Wheeler, Maria (1997) *A Treasure Chest of Behavioral Strategies for Individuals with Autism.* Arlington, TX: Future Horizons, Inc.

Hodgdon, Linda (1999) *Solving Behavior Problems in Autism.* Troy, MI: Quirk Roberts Publishing.

Schopler, Eric (ed) (1995) *Parent Survival Manual: A Guide to Crisis Resolution in Autism and Related Developmental Disorders.* New York: Plenum Press.

Sensory books

Kranowitz, Carol and Miller, Lucy (2005) *The Out-of-Sync Child,* revised edition. New York: Perigee Books.

Yack, Ellen, Aquilla, Paula and Sutton, Shirley (2002) *Building Bridges Through Sensory Integration Therapy for Children with Autism and Other Pervasive Developmental Disorders,* second edition. Las Vegas: Sensory Resources.

Lots of ideas for dealing with specific tasks, such as self-care tasks.

Finding doctors and dentists experienced in working with children with special needs

Consult local chapters of disability organizations to locate doctors experienced with those with disabilities.

Sibling resources

Books

Hames, Annette and McCaffrey, Monica (eds) (2005) *Special Brothers and Sisters: Stories and Tips for Siblings of Children with Special Needs, Disability or Serious Illness.* London: Jessica Kingsley Publishers.

Meyer, Donald J. and Vadasy, Patricia (1996) *Living with a Brother or Sister with Special Needs: A Book for Sibs,* 2nd revised edition. Seattle, WA: University of Washington Press.

Meyer, Donald (ed), and drawings by Carry Pillo (1997) *Views from Our Shoes: Growing Up with a Brother or Sister with Special Needs.* Bethesda, MD: Woodbine House.

Meyer, Donald (ed) (2005) *The Sibling Slam Book: What It's Really Like to Have a Brother or Sister with Special Needs.* Bethesda, MD: Woodbine House.

Website

www.sibs.org.uk

An organization in the UK for siblings of any age of those with special needs, disability or chronic illness. It provides support and information, sponsors workshops and conferences, and sets up networks of adult siblings.

Listservs

For siblings to connect with each other.

www.thearc.org/siblingsupport/sibkids-listserv (for younger siblings of those with special needs)

www.thearc.org/siblingsupport/sibnet-listserv (for adult siblings of those with special needs)

Index